Lecture Notes in Economics and Mathematical Systems

For information about Vols. 1–156, please contact your bookseller or Springer-Verlag

Vol. 157: Optimization and Operations Research. Proceedings 1977. Edited by R. Henn, B. Korte, and W. Oettli. VI, 270 pages. 1978.

Vol. 158: L. J. Cherene, Set Valued Dynamical Systems and Economic Flow. VIII, 83 pages. 1978.

Vol. 159: Some Aspects of the Foundations of General Equilibrium Theory: The Posthumous Papers of Peter J. Kalman. Edited by J. Green. VI, 167 pages. 1978.

Vol. 160: Integer Programming and Related Areas. A Classified Bibliography. Edited by D. Hausmann. XIV, 314 pages. 1978.

Vol. 161: M. J. Beckmann, Rank in Organizations. VIII, 164 pages. 1978.

Vol. 162: Recent Developments in Variable Structure Systems, Economics and Biology. Proceedings 1977. Edited by R. R. Mohler and A. Ruberti. VI, 326 pages. 1978.

Vol. 163: G. Fandel, Optimale Entscheidungen in Organisationen. VI, 143 Seiten. 1979.

Vol. 164: C. L. Hwang and A. S. M. Masud, Multiple Objective Decision Making – Methods and Applications. A State-of-the-Art Survey. XII, 351 pages. 1979.

Vol. 165: A. Maravall, Identification in Dynamic Shock-Error Models. VIII, 158 pages. 1979.

Vol. 166: R. Cuninghame-Green, Minimax Algebra. XI, 258 pages. 1979.

Vol. 167: M. Faber, Introduction to Modern Austrian Capital Theory. X, 196 pages. 1979.

Vol. 168: Convex Analysis and Mathematical Economics. Proceedings 1978. Edited by J. Kriens. V, 136 pages. 1979.

Vol. 169: A. Rapoport et al., Coalition Formation by Sophisticated Players. VII, 170 pages. 1979.

Vol. 170: A. E. Roth, Axiomatic Models of Bargaining. V, 121 pages. 1979.

Vol. 171: G. F. Newell, Approximate Behavior of Tandem Queues. XI, 410 pages. 1979.

Vol. 172: K. Neumann and U. Steinhardt, GERT Networks and the Time-Oriented Evaluation of Projects. 268 pages. 1979.

Vol. 173: S. Erlander, Optimal Spatial Interaction and the Gravity Model. VII, 107 pages. 1980.

Vol. 174: Extremal Methods and Systems Analysis. Edited by A. V. Fiacco and K. O. Kortanek. XI, 545 pages. 1980.

Vol. 175: S. K. Srinivasan and R. Subramanian, Probabilistic Analysis of Redundant Systems. VII, 356 pages. 1980.

Vol. 176: R. Färe, Laws of Diminishing Returns. VIII, 97 pages. 1980.

Vol. 177: Multiple Criteria Decision Making-Theory and Application. Proceedings, 1979. Edited by G. Fandel and T. Gal. XVI, 570 pages. 1980.

Vol. 178: M. N. Bhattacharyya, Comparison of Box-Jenkins and Bonn Monetary Model Prediction Performance. VII, 146 pages. 1980.

Vol. 179: Recent Results in Stochastic Programming. Proceedings, 1979. Edited by P. Kall and A. Prékopa. IX, 237 pages. 1980.

Vol. 180: J. F. Brotchie, J. W. Dickey and R. Sharpe, TOPAZ – General Planning Technique and its Applications at the Regional, Urban, and Facility Planning Levels. VII, 356 pages. 1980.

Vol. 181: H. D. Sherali and C. M. Shetty, Optimization with Disjunctive Constraints. VIII, 156 pages. 1980.

Vol. 182: J. Wolters, Stochastic Dynamic Properties of Linear Econometric Models. VIII, 154 pages. 1980.

Vol. 183: K. Schittkowski, Nonlinear Programming Codes. VIII, 242 pages. 1980.

Vol. 184: R. E. Burkard and U. Derigs, Assignment and Matching Problems: Solution Methods with FORTRAN-Programs. VIII, 148 pages. 1980.

Vol. 185: C. C. von Weizsäcker, Barriers to Entry. VI, 220 pages. 1980.

Vol. 186: Ch.-L. Hwang and K. Yoon, Multiple Attribute Decision Making – Methods and Applications. A State-of-the-Art-Survey. XI, 259 pages. 1981.

Vol. 187: W. Hock, K. Schittkowski, Test Examples for Nonlinear Programming Codes. V. 178 pages. 1981.

Vol. 188: D. Bös, Economic Theory of Public Enterprise. VII, 142 pages. 1981.

Vol. 189: A. P. Lüthi, Messung wirtschaftlicher Ungleichheit. IX, 287 pages. 1981.

Vol. 190: J. N. Morse, Organizations: Multiple Agents with Multiple Criteria. Proceedings, 1980. VI, 509 pages. 1981.

Vol. 191: H. R. Sneessens, Theory and Estimation of Macroeconomic Rationing Models. VII, 138 pages. 1981.

Vol. 192: H. J. Bierens: Robust Methods and Asymptotic Theory in Nonlinear Econometrics. IX, 198 pages. 1981.

Vol. 193: J. K. Sengupta, Optimal Decisions under Uncertainty. VII, 156 pages. 1981.

Vol. 194: R. W. Shephard, Cost and Production Functions. XI; 104 pages. 1981.

Vol. 195: H. W. Ursprung, Die elementare Katastrophentheorie. Eine Darstellung aus der Sicht der Ökonomie. VII, 332 pages. 1982.

Vol. 196: M. Nermuth, Information Structures in Economics. VIII, 236 pages. 1982.

Vol. 197: Integer Programming and Related Areas. A Classified Bibliography. 1978 – 1981. Edited by R. von Randow. XIV, 338 pages. 1982.

Vol. 198: P. Zweifel, Ein ökonomisches Modell des Arztverhaltens. XIX, 392 Seiten. 1982.

Vol. 199: Evaluating Mathematical Programming Techniques. Proceedings, 1981. Edited by J.M. Mulvey. XI, 379 pages. 1982.

Vol. 200: The Resource Sector in an Open Economy. Edited by H. Siebert. IX, 161 pages. 1984.

Vol. 201: P. M. C. de Boer, Price Effects in Input-Output-Relations: A Theoretical and Empirical Study for the Netherlands 1949–1967. X, 140 pages. 1982.

Vol. 202: U. Witt, J. Perske, SMS – A Program Package for Simulation and Gaming of Stochastic Market Processes and Learning Behavior. VII, 266 pages. 1982.

Vol. 203: Compilation of Input-Output Tables. Proceedings, 1981. Edited by J. V. Skolka. VII, 307 pages. 1982.

Vol. 204: K. C. Mosler, Entscheidungsregeln bei Risiko: Multivariate stochastische Dominanz. VII, 172 Seiten. 1982.

Vol. 205: R. Ramanathan, Introduction to the Theory of Economic Growth. IX, 347 pages. 1982.

Vol. 206: M. H. Karwan, V. Lotfi, J. Telgen, and S. Zionts, Redundancy in Mathematical Programming. VII, 286 pages. 1983.

Vol. 207: Y. Fujimori, Modern Analysis of Value Theory. X, 165 pages. 1982.

Vol. 208: Econometric Decision Models. Proceedings, 1981. Edited by J. Gruber. VI, 364 pages. 1983.

Vol. 209: Essays and Surveys on Multiple Criteria Decision Making. Proceedings, 1982. Edited by P. Hansen. VII, 441 pages. 1983.

Vol. 210: Technology, Organization and Economic Structure. Edited by R. Sato and M. J. Beckmann. VIII, 195 pages. 1983.

continuation on page 151

Lecture Notes
in Economics and
Mathematical Systems

Managing Editors: M. Beckmann and W. Krelle

303

Francis X. Diebold

Empirical Modeling of Exchange Rate Dynamics

Springer-Verlag
Berlin Heidelberg New York London Paris Tokyo

Managing Editors

Prof. Dr. M. Beckmann
Brown University
Providence, RI 02912, USA

Prof. Dr. W. Krelle
Institut für Gesellschafts- und Wirtschaftswissenschaften
der Universität Bonn
Adenauerallee 24–42, D-5300 Bonn, FRG

Author

Dr. Francis X. Diebold
Board of Governors of the Federal Reserve System
Division of Research and Statistics, 20th and Constitution Ave., NW
Washington, DC 20551, USA

ISBN-13: 978-3-540-18966-4 e-ISBN-13: 978-3-642-45641-1
DOI: 10.1007/978-3-642-45641-1

To my wife, Susan

and my parents, Frank and Catherine

Preface

The work upon which this book is based was completed largely at the University of Pennsylvania, and incorporates the explicit or implicit influence of numerous individuals there. In particular, I wish to thank Lawrence Klein, Marc Nerlove, Peter Pauly and Glenn Rudebusch, as well as Albert Ando, Alok Bhargava, David Cass, Patrick DeGraba, Regina Forlano, Claudia Goldin, Jevons Lee, Richard Marston, Roberto Mariano, Paul Shaman, Allen Schirm, Robin Sickles, Robert Summers, and Asad Zaman.

Expert and meticulous word processing was performed at various stages by Lisa Bonner, Lynn Costello, Madelene Dyckman, and Ann Fasciolo. Susan Quant provided gregarious assistance at all stages.

My colleagues at the Federal Reserve, in particular Peter Tinsley and Paul Spindt, have provided a stimulating environment in which to continue this research.

I am certain that the help of the above individuals has led to a vastly improved monograph. I, not they, bear full responsibility for all remaining errors, inaccuracies, and omissions.

F.X.D.

Washington, DC
1987

TABLE OF CONTENTS

Chapter One: Introduction

Structural exchange rate modeling has proven extremely difficult during the recent post-1973 float. The disappointment climaxed with the papers of Meese and Rogoff (1983a, 1983b), who showed that a "naive" random walk model distinctly dominated received theoretical models in terms of predictive performance for the major dollar spot rates. One purpose of this monograph is to seek the reasons for this failure by exploring the temporal behavior of seven major dollar exchange rates using nonstructural time-series methods.

The Meese-Rogoff finding does not mean that exchange rates evolve as random walks; rather it simply means that the random walk is a better stochastic approximation than any of their other candidate models. In this monograph, we use optimal model specification techniques, including formal unit root tests which allow for trend, and find that all of the exchange rates studied do in fact evolve as random walks or random walks with drift (to a very close approximation). This result is consistent with efficient asset markets, and provides an explanation for the Meese-Rogoff results.

Far more subtle forces are at work, however, which lead to interesting econometric problems and have implications for the measurement of exchange rate volatility and moment structure. It is shown that all exchange rates display substantial conditional heteroskedasticity. A particularly reasonable parameterization of this conditional heteroskedasticity, which captures the observed clustering of prediction error variances, is developed in Chapter 2. Estimation and hypothesis testing of this ARCH (Autoregressive Conditional Heteroskedasticity) model are treated in depth, and it is shown that an independent, identically distributed structure in first differences (i.e., a random walk) emerges only as a very special case. What appear to be random walks (in terms of conditional mean behavior) are not random walks at all; successive first-differenced observations, while uncorrelated, are not independent. Again, the nature of this serial dependence is studied in detail. The problem of testing for serial correlation in the presence of ARCH is also treated, and the asymptotic distributions of some important serial correlation test statistics are characterized in the presence of ARCH.

Another insight of Chapter 2 is that, if ARCH is present, it leads to unconditionally leptokurtic exchange rate distributions, even though the conditional distribution is Gaussian. This fact is used to explain the well-known fat-tailed unconditional distributions of exchange rate movements. In addition, central limit theorems for temporal aggregation of ARCH processes are proved, which show that the unconditional density approaches normality as observational frequency decreases.

In summary, then, groundwork is laid in Chapter 2 via detailed characterization of conditional and unconditional ARCH moment structures, treatment of hypothesis testing for ARCH effects and estimation of ARCH models, central limit theorems for temporal aggregation of ARCH processes (in spite of the fact that successive observations are not independent), and derivation of the properties of serial correlation tests in the presence of ARCH. The results are used and refined in later chapters to study the nature of nominal and real exchange rate movements.

In Chapter 3, the univariate stochastic structures of seven major weekly dollar spot exchange rates are studied; each rate is found to possess one (and only one) unit root in its autoregressive lag operator polynomial and strong ARCH effects. Maximum likelihood estimates of the ARCH model parameters are obtained for each exchange rate. They are then used to construct meaningful measures of exchange rate volatility which are compared to various measures commonly used in the literature. In addition to providing useful volatility measures and explaining the leptokurtosis found in each exchange rate, it is shown that the time-varying conditional variances may be used to construct superior prediction intervals, which are "tighter" in more tranquil times and "wider" in more volatile times than prediction intervals obtained via classical methods.

In Chapter 4, the data are aggregated to monthly frequency, and the theoretical results of Chapter 2 are verified. Specifically, the conditional mean behavior of each rate is still well described by a random walk (with larger innovation variance, due to the lower frequency of observation). Kurtosis is substantially reduced for each currency, as are ARCH effects, confirming the predictions of the earlier limit theorems. Neither ARCH nor the associated leptokurtosis is completely eliminated, however.

Real exchange rates are examined in Chapter 5, leading to tests of absolute and relative purchasing power parity (PPP) that simultaneously control for residual ARCH effects. The formal unit root tests which are used facilitate rigorous analysis of both CPI- and WPI-based real exchange rates. While absolute PPP is decisively rejected, relative PPP is accepted, apart from low-order ARCH effects in the residuals. As a precursor to the PPP analysis, the relations between three important parity conditions (uncovered interest parity, purchasing power parity, and real interest parity) are characterized and related to recent literature. Finally, the nature and implications of long-run versus short-run deviations from PPP are considered.

Chapter Two: Conditional Heteroskedasticity in Economic Time Series

2.1) Introduction and Summary

In this chapter we introduce a model of autoregressive conditional heteroskedasticity (ARCH). The model is motivated explicitly by considerations arising in a time-series context, and it will play a key role in the analysis of dollar spot exchange rates of later chapters. In section 2.2, we begin by developing a parameterization of the ARCH model introduced by Engle (1982b) and comparing it to more standard models of conditonal heteroskedasticity which, while of great use in a cross-sectional context, are difficult to apply and therefore of limited value in a time-series environment. It is argued that such a model represents a natural and powerful generalization of the "classical" time-series models which have proved so useful in econometrics, such as the class of autoregressive moving average (ARMA) processes. More generally, in fact, the allowance for possible conditional heteroskedasticity provides a generalization of the entire class of linearly regular covariance-stationary stochastic processes. The motivation and properties of ARCH processes are developed in detail. It is shown that a classical process consisting of independent identically distributed (iid) observations, or a regression or time-series model with iid disturbances, arises as a special case. The autoregressive model with conditionally heteroskedastic disturbances is treated in depth, both for illustration and to lay the foundation for the work of later chapters. In particular, both the conditional and unconditional moment structures are treated.

Section 2.3 considers the temporal aggregation of ARCH processes. Central limit theorems are proved which show that the leptokurtic unconditional densities of ARCH processes approach normality when aggregated, in spite of the fact that successive observations are <u>not</u> independent. As a corollary, it is shown that convergence to normality coincides with diminishing ARCH effects, so that temporal aggregation of ARCH processes produces independent, identically distributed Gaussian white noise in the limit. This unifies the results of later chapters, in which we see that while strong

ARCH effects are found in all high-frequency dollar spot exchange rates, they diminish with frequency of observation. Similarly, while high-frequency exchange rates are highly leptokurtic, convergence to normality is seen as observational frequency decreases.

Section 2.4 treats estimation and hypothesis testing in ARCH models, and section 2.5 treats associated problems of testing for serial correlation in the presence of conditonal heteroskedasticity. Specifically, the properties of the Bartlett standard errors and the Box-Pierce and Box-Ljung "portmanteau" tests are characterized in the presence of ARCH. It is shown that all of the tests have empirical size larger than nominal size, leading to larger than nominal probability of type I error. Appropriate correction factors are developed analytically and shown to perform very well in a numerical example. Again, the results have substantive implications in terms of the analysis of later chapters, in which we are constantly testing for exchange rate serial correlation in the presence of ARCH. Concluding remarks are given in section 2.6.

2.2) Autoregressive Conditionally Heteroskedastic Processes

2.2.1) Conditional Moment Structure

Consider a time series $\{\varepsilon_t\}$ such that :

$$(\varepsilon_t|\ \varepsilon_{t-1},\ \ldots,\ \varepsilon_{t-p}) \sim N(0,\sigma_t^2)$$

$$\sigma_t^2 = f(\varepsilon_{t-1}\ \ldots,\ \varepsilon_{t-p}).$$

Such processes, first studied by Engle (1982b), display what is known as autoregressive conditional heteroskedasticity (ARCH). The process is defined in terms of the conditional (as opposed to unconditional) density, and has the interesting property that the conditional variance may move over time, being a function of p past realized innovations. We therefore denote the model by ARCH(p). To make the model useful, the funcion f(•) must be parameterized, and conditions must be imposed to guarantee positive conditional (and unconditional) variances.

Throughout this book we adopt the following natural parameterization:

$$(\varepsilon_t | \varepsilon_{t-1}, \ldots, \varepsilon_{t-p}) \sim N(o, \sigma_t^2),$$

$$\sigma_t^2 = \alpha_0 + \sum_{i=1}^{p} \alpha_i \varepsilon_{t-i}^2$$

$$\equiv Z_t \alpha$$

where:

$Z_t = (1, \varepsilon_{t-1}^2, \ldots, \varepsilon_{t-p}^2)$

$\alpha = (\alpha_0, \ldots, \alpha_p)'$

$\alpha_0 > 0, \alpha_i \geq 0, i = 1, \ldots, p$.

The conditional variance of ε_t is allowed to vary over time as a linear function of past squared realizations. In the expected value sense, then, today's variability depends linearly on yesterday's variability, so that large changes tend to be followed by large changes, and small by small, of <u>either sign</u>. Such temporal clustering of prediction error variances has been well documented in the classic work on stochastic generating mechanisms for financial markets such as Fama (1965, 1976) and Mandelbrot (1963). (McNees (1979) discusses the same issues in terms of forecast error variance clustering in the context of econometric prediction.) The ARCH model formalizes this phenomenon and enables us to test for it rigorously since the iid model is nested within the ARCH model, occurring when $\alpha_1 = \alpha_2 = \ldots = \alpha_p = 0$.

Comparison with a pth-order zero-mean stationary autoregressive model is instructive. Suppose:

$$\varepsilon_t | \varepsilon_{t-1}, \ldots, \varepsilon_{t-p} \sim N(\mu_t, \sigma^2)$$

$$\mu_t = \rho_1 \varepsilon_{t-1} + \ldots + \rho_p \varepsilon_{t-p}$$

$$= R(L) \varepsilon_t$$

where all roots of $[1 - R(L)]$ lie outside the unit circle. Like the ARCH model, this model is also defined in terms of the conditional distribution. The evolution of conditional moments is exactly the converse, however: the conditional mean evolves in an autoregressive fashion, while the conditional variance is held fixed. The desirability of models that allow for evolution of both conditional means and conditional variances is obvious. Before proceeding to such models, however, we pause to contrast the ARCH model with a standard "textbook" approach to conditional heteroskedasticity. Suppose that:

$$\varepsilon_t \mid \Omega_t \sim N(0, \sigma_t^2)$$

$$\sigma_t^2 = \exp(Z_t \alpha)$$

$$= \exp(\alpha_1) \exp(\alpha_2 Z_{t2}) \cdots \exp(\alpha_p Z_{tp})$$

where Ω_t is the time-t information set, Z_t is a (1 x p) vector of exogenous variables that explain the variance ($Z_{t1} = 1$ for all t), and α is a (p x 1) parameter vector. (The classical iid structure emerges when $\alpha = (\alpha_1, 0, \ldots, 0)$.) For example, the common specification

$$\varepsilon_t \sim N(0, \sigma_t^2)$$

$$\sigma_t^2 = \sigma_0^2 \, x_{it}^s ,$$

where x_i is one of the regressors in an equation of which ε_t is the disturbance, emerges when $p = 2$, $Z_t = (1, \ln x_{it})$ and $\alpha = (\ln \sigma_0^2, s)'$. The problem with such an approach is that the appropriate set of forcing variables (Z) for the variance is rarely known in the context of the analysis of economic time series (as opposed to cross sections). The ARCH model, on the other hand, may be viewed as a general approximation to conditional heteroskedasticity of unknown form.

2.2.2) Unconditional Moment Structure

The unconditional moment structure of ARCH processes is very interesting. By symmetry, all odd-ordered moments are zero. Even-ordered moments may or may not exist (i.e. may or may not be finite). Nemec (1985) has shown that no nondegenerate ARCH process has finite moments of all orders, and that progressively more stringent requirements must be satisfied for existence of progressively higher order moments.

For example, Engle (1982b) has shown that for an ARCH(p) process, the unconditional variance is finite if $\sum_{i=1}^{p} \alpha_i < 1$. Similarly, Milhoj (1985) shows that the unconditional fourth moment exists if:

$$3\, a' \, (I-\psi)^{-1} \, a < 1$$

where $a' = (\alpha_1, \ldots, \alpha_p)$ and $\underset{(p\times p)}{\psi}$ is defined by $\psi_{ij} = \alpha_{i+j} + \alpha_{i-j}$ where we set $\alpha_k = 0$ for $k \le 0$ and $k > p$.

Actual calculation of the unconditional moments is done by applying the law of iterated expectations. Consider, for example, the ARCH (1) process:

$$\varepsilon_t \mid \varepsilon_{t-1} \sim N(0, \sigma_t^2)$$

$$\sigma_t^2 = \alpha_0 + \alpha_1 \, \varepsilon_{t-1}^2$$

$$\alpha_0 > 0, \quad 0 \le \alpha_1 < 1 .$$

Rewrite the variance equation as:

$$E(\varepsilon_t^2 \mid \varepsilon_{t-1}) = \alpha_0 + \alpha_1 \, \varepsilon_{t-1}^2 .$$

Taking expectations of both sides gives:

$$\sigma^2 = \alpha_0 + \alpha_1 \sigma^2 .$$

Thus,

$$\sigma^2 = \frac{\alpha_0}{1 - \alpha_1} .$$

More generally, it can be shown that:

$$\sigma^2 = \frac{\alpha_0}{1 - \sum_{i=1}^{p} \alpha_i}$$

for an ARCH(p) process.

Conditional normality may be similarly exploited for the calculation of unconditional fourth moments. Consider again the first order model. Then because of conditional normality, we have:

$$E(\varepsilon_t^4 \mid \varepsilon_{t-1}) = 3\,\sigma_t^4 = 3(\alpha_0 + \alpha_1\,\varepsilon_{t-1}^2)^2 .$$

Thus, taking expectations of both sides:

$$\mu_4 = 3\,E(\alpha_0 + \alpha_1\,\varepsilon_{t-1}^2)^2$$

$$= 3\,E(\alpha_0^2 + \alpha_1^2\,\varepsilon_{t-1}^4 + 2\alpha_0\,\alpha_1\,\varepsilon_{t-1}^2)$$

$$= 3\,(\alpha_0^2 + \alpha_1^2\,\mu_4 + 2\alpha_0^2\,\alpha_1 \,/\, (1-\alpha_1)\,)$$

and therefore:

$$\mu_4 = \frac{3\,\alpha_0^2\,(1+\alpha_1)}{(1-\alpha_1)\,(1-3\,\alpha_1^2)} .$$

More generally, we can modify a result of Milhoj (1985) to obtain a general expression for the fourth moment of an ARCH(p) process. Milhoj considers the process $\{X_t^2\}$, where $\{X_t\}$ is ARCH(p) and shows that:

$$\gamma_{X^2}(0) = E(X_t^2 - EX_t^2)^2$$

$$= \frac{2\,\sigma^4}{1 - 3\,a'\,(I-\psi)^{-1}a}$$

$$= \frac{2\,\mu_2^2}{1 - 3\,a'\,(I-\psi)^{-1}\,a} .$$

But the will should note at once that:

$$\gamma_{X^2}(0) = E(X_t^2 - \mu_2)^2$$

$$= E\,X_t^4 - \sigma^4$$

$$= \mu_4 - \mu_2^2 .$$

Thus,

$$\mu_4 = \frac{2\,\mu_2^{\,2}}{1 - 3\,a'\,(I - \psi)^{-1}a} + \mu_2^{\,2} ,$$

where $$\mu_2 = \frac{\alpha_0}{1 - \sum_{i-1}^{p} \alpha_i} .$$

This brings us to a very important result: ARCH processes are leptokurtic, or "fat-tailed", relative to the normal. This is stated formally below.

Theorem

Consider an ARCH(p) process with

$$\alpha_0 > 0,\ \alpha_i > 0,\ i = 1, \ldots, p,\ \sum_{i=1}^{p} \alpha_i < 1,$$

and

$$3\,a'\,(I - \psi)^{-1}a < 1 .$$

Such a process is leptokurtic.

Proof

$$\text{Kurtosis} = \frac{\mu_4}{\mu_2^{\,2}} = \frac{2}{1 - 3\,a'\,(I - \psi)^{-1}a} + 1 .$$

The facts that $\alpha_i > 0$ $i = 1, \ldots, p$ and $\sum_{i=1}^{p} \alpha_i < 1$ guarantee that

$$\det\,(I - \psi) > 0 .$$

Thus,

$$0 < 3\,a'\,(I - \psi)^{-1}a < 1 ,$$

so,

$$\frac{2}{1 - 3\,a'\,(I - \psi)^{-1}a} > 2 ,$$

which means that the kurtosis must be greater than three. (Kurtosis of three corresponds to normality.) **QED**

Finally, as an example of how processes which display serial correlation in the conditional mean can be fruitfully combined with ARCH processes (allowing for serial correlation in the conditional variance), we consider the following AR (1) process with ARCH (1) disturbances:

$$y_t = \rho\, y_{t-1} + \varepsilon_t$$

$$\varepsilon_t \mid \varepsilon_{t-1} \sim N(0, \sigma_t^2)$$

$$\sigma_t^2 = \alpha_0 + \alpha_1\, \varepsilon_{t-1}^2$$

$$|\rho| < 1,\ 0 \leq \alpha_1 \leq 1/\sqrt{3},\ \alpha_0 > 0 .$$

The unconditional density of the innovation ε is easily seen to have all odd-ordered moments equal to zero, second moment $\alpha_0 / (1 - \alpha_1)$, and fourth moment:

$$\frac{3\, \alpha_0^2\, (1 + \alpha_1)}{(1 - \alpha_1)\, (1 - 3\, \alpha_1^2)} .$$

The kurtosis is therefore:

$$\frac{3\, (1 + \alpha_1)\, (1 - \alpha_1)}{(1 - 3\, \alpha_1^2)} > 3$$

so that the density is fat-tailed relative to the normal. Thus, while the conditional density of y_t is normal with mean ρy_{t-1} and variance $\alpha_0 + \alpha_1\, \varepsilon_{t-1}^2$, its unconditional density is leptokurtic with mean zero and variance:

$$\frac{\alpha_0}{(1 - \alpha_1)\, (1 - \rho^2)} .$$

2.3) Temporal Aggregation of ARCH Processes

Consider a time series $\{y_t\}_{t=1}^{T}$, obeying an ARCH probability law, where t = 1, 2, 3, ... is some "fundamental" time scale. Now form the m-period temporal aggregate:

$$S_t^m = \sum_{i=0}^{m-1} y_{t-i}, \quad t = m, 2m, 3m, \ldots .$$

We write the time series as $\{S_t^m\}_{t=1}^{T/m,m}$, or $\{S_{t^*}\}_{t^*=1}^{T/m}$, where t = km is equivalent to t^* = k. For example, if $\{D_t\}_{t=1}^{T}$, is a daily time series, then the series of weekly returns corresponds to the m = 5 day aggregate $\{W_{t^*}\}_{t^*=1}^{T/5}$,

where:

$$W_t = \sum_{i=0}^{4} D_{t-i} = D_t + D_{t-1} + \ldots + D_{t-4}, \quad t = m, 2m, \ldots$$

and t = k m <=> t* = k.

We are interested in the properties of such aggregates as $m \to \infty$. In other words, we ask "Does S_t^m have a limiting distribution as $m \to \infty$, and if so, what is it?" Unfortunately, standard central limit theory does not apply because, as shown above, the elements of $\{y_t\}$ are not independent. We can, however, exploit a theorem of White (1984) for regression with dependent identically (unconditionally) distributed observations to characterize the limiting distribution of the aggregate. We reproduce it here in a slightly different notation.

Theorem

Given:

(i) $y = X\beta_0 + \varepsilon$;

(ii) $\{(X_t, \varepsilon_t)'\}$ is a stationary ergodic sequence;

(iii) (a) $E(X_{0hi}\varepsilon_{0h} | \Omega_{-r}) \xrightarrow{q.m.} 0$ as $r \to \infty$, where $\{\Omega_t\}$ is adapted to $\{X_{thi}\varepsilon_{th}\}$, h = 1, ..., P, i = 1, ..., k;

(b) $E\,|X_{thi}\,\varepsilon_{th}|^2 < \infty$, $h = 1, \ldots, P$, $i = 1, \ldots, k$;

(c) $V_m = \text{var}\,(m^{-1/2} X'\varepsilon)$ is uniformly positive definite;

(d) Define $\Pi_{0hij} \equiv E(X_{0hi}\varepsilon_{0h}|\Omega_{-j}) - E\,(X_{0hi}\varepsilon_{0h}|\Omega_{-j-1})$, $h = 1, \ldots, p$, $i = 1, \ldots, k$. For $h = 1, \ldots, p$, $i = 1, \ldots, k$, assume that $\Sigma_{j=0}^{\infty}(\text{var}\,\Pi_{0hij})^{1/2} < \infty$.

(iv) (a) $E|X_{thi}|^2 < \infty$, $h = 1, \ldots, p$, $i = 1, \ldots, k$;

(b) $M \equiv E(X_t'X_t)$ is positive definite;

Then $V_m \to V$ finite and positive definite as $m \to \infty$, and:

$$D^{-1/2}\sqrt{m}(\hat{\beta}_n - \beta_0) \overset{a}{\sim} N\,(0,I), ,$$

where $D = M^{-1}VM^{-1}$.

Suppose in addition that

(v) There exists $\hat{V}_m$ symmetric and positive semidefinite such that $\hat{V}_m - V_m \overset{p}{\to} 0$.

Then $\hat{D}_m - D \overset{p}{\to} 0$, where $\hat{D}_m = (X'X/m)^{-1}\,\hat{V}_m(X'X/m)^{-1}$.

Consider first the case in which y_t follows a pure ARCH(p) process, and write $y = X\beta + \varepsilon$, where X is simply a column vector of ones. The reader may verify that conditions (i) - (iv) are satisfied, where $V_m = V = \sigma^2$ for all sample sizes m, M = 1, and σ^2 is the unconditional variance of ε_t given by:

$$\frac{\alpha_0}{1 - \sum_{i=1}^{p} \alpha_i}\,.$$

Thus, $D = V = \sigma^2$ and we have:

$$\frac{1}{\sigma}\sqrt{m}\,(\hat{\beta}_m - \beta_0) \overset{a}{\sim} N\,(0,1)$$

or

$$(\hat{\beta}_m - \beta_0) \overset{a}{\sim} N\,(0, \frac{\sigma^2}{m}).$$

Under our assumptions, however, $\beta_0 = 0$, and, of course,

$$\hat{\beta}_m = (X'X)^{-1} X'y = \frac{1}{m} \sum_{t=1}^{m} y_t .$$

Thus,

$$\frac{1}{m} \sum_{t=1}^{m} y_t \overset{a}{\sim} N\left(0, \frac{\sigma^2}{m}\right),$$

so,

$$\sum_{t=1}^{m} y_t \overset{a}{\sim} N(0, m\sigma^2).$$

We have just proved the following proposition.

Proposition 2.1

If a time series $\{y_t\}$ follows a zero mean pth order ARCH process with $\sum_{i=1}^{p} \alpha_i < 1$, then the aggregated series $\{S^m_{t*}\}$ has an unconditional normal distribution as $m \to \infty$.

Now assume that y_t is not a pure ARCH process; rather, assume a Pth order autoregression (about a possibly nonzero mean) with pth order ARCH disturbances. Consider once again the representation:

$$y = X\beta + \varepsilon$$

where $X = (1,\ldots,1)'$ and ε is a zero-mean AR-ARCH (P,p) process. The regularity conditions of the White theorem are again satisfied, with:

$$V_m = \text{var}\,(m^{-1/2} X'\varepsilon) = \text{var}\,(m^{-1/2} \sum_{t=1}^{m} \varepsilon_t)$$

$$= m^{-1} \sum_{t=1}^{m} \frac{\alpha_0}{(1 - \Sigma\, \alpha_i)(1 - \Sigma\, \phi_j \rho_j)}$$

$$= \frac{\alpha_0}{(1 - \Sigma\, \alpha_i)(1 - \Sigma\, \phi_j \rho_j)} = V$$

where ρ_i, i = 1...P is the ith autocorrelation of the AR(P) process (with parameters $\phi_1, \ldots, \phi_P$) which describes the evolution of the conditional mean of y. As before, M = 1, and D = V. We therefore have:

$$\left(\frac{\alpha_0}{(1 - \Sigma \alpha_i)(1 - \Sigma \phi_j \rho_j)}\right)^{-1/2} \sqrt{m}\ (\hat{\beta}_m - \beta_0) \overset{a}{\sim} N\ (0,1),$$

or:

$$\hat{\beta}_m \overset{a}{\sim} N\ \left(\beta_0, \frac{\alpha_0}{m\ (1 - \Sigma \alpha_i)(1 - \Sigma \phi_j \rho_j)}\right).$$

Finally, then,

$$\sum_{t=1}^{m} y_t \overset{a}{\sim} N\ \left(m\beta_0, \frac{m\alpha_0}{(1 - \Sigma \alpha_i)(1 - \Sigma \phi_j \rho_j)}\right).$$

This establishes the following proposition.

Proposition 2.2:

If a time series $\{y_t\}$ follows an AR-ARCH(P,p) process about a (possibly) nonzero mean, and $\Sigma \alpha_i < 1$, then the aggregated series $\{S^m_{t^*}\}$ has an unconditional normal distribution as $m \to \infty$.

To illustrate the results, the simple first order ARCH process:

$$y_t = N_t\ (0,1)(.5 + .5\ y_{t-1}^2)^{1/2}$$

is used. A sufficiently large realization is obtained such that 5,000 observations on the aggregated series $\{S^m_t\}$ are available, for m = 0, 4, 12, 25, 50, and 100. In Figure 2.1, we plot kurtosis as a function of m; the convergence to normality is evident at once. The convergence to normality is also confirmed by a wide range of other diagnostics such as Kolmogorov's D, normal probability plots, and the percentiles of the standardized distribution. The kurtosis corresponding to m = 1 (no aggregation) is 9.011, which matches very closely the analytical kurtosis of:

$$\frac{3\ (1 - \alpha_1)^2}{1 - 3\ \alpha_1^2} = 9.0\ .$$

As we aggregate, both the kurtosis and the studentized range drop monotonically until respective values of 3.226 and 9.5 are obtained for m = 100. The skewness, of course, stays close to zero throughout.

2.4) Estimation and Hypothesis Testing

First note that the log likelihood is given by:

$$\ln L = \text{const} - \sum_{t=1}^{T} \ln\ (Z_t\ \alpha)^{1/2} - 1/2 \sum_{t=1}^{T} \frac{\varepsilon_t^2}{Z_t\ \alpha}\ .$$

We can use this likelihood function to obtain consistent, asymptotically efficient parameter estimates, as well as a Lagrange multiplier test of the null hypothesis of no ARCH effects. In what follows it will prove useful to model a time series $\{y_t\}$, allowing for a time-varying conditional mean, which we denote by $X_t\beta$. The X's may be composed of both exogenous and lagged dependent variables; later, we will explicitly model third order autoregressions with ARCH innovations. In any case, X is taken to be a (T x K) matrix, while β is a (K x 1) vector of parameters. The log likelihood function is then:

$$\ln L(\beta,\ \alpha;\ y,\ X) = \text{const} - \sum_{t=1}^{T} \ln\ \sigma_t - \frac{1}{2} \sum_{t=1}^{T} \frac{\varepsilon_t^2}{\sigma_t^2}\ ,$$

where $\varepsilon_t \equiv y_t - X_t B$.

The likelihood ratio (LR) test of the null hypothesis $\alpha_1 = \cdots = \alpha_p = 0$ is then given by:

$$- 2 \ln(L_\omega(\beta, \alpha)/L_\Omega(\beta,\alpha)) \overset{asy}{\sim} \chi_p^2 .$$

The LR test requires estimates under both the null and alternative, of course, so that an LM test which requires estimates only under the null may serve as a convenient preliminary diagnostic. The LM statistic is:

$$LM = d'I^{\alpha\alpha} d \overset{asy}{\sim} \chi_p^2$$

where d is the score vector with respect to α, $\frac{\partial \ln L}{\partial \alpha}$, $I^{\alpha\alpha}$ is the $\alpha\alpha$ block of the inverse of the information matrix, and both d and $I^{\alpha\alpha}$ are evaluated under the null.

To obtain these, rewrite the likelihood function as:

$$\ln L = \text{const} - \Sigma \ln(Z_t\alpha)^{1/2} - \frac{1}{2} \Sigma \frac{(y_t - X_t\beta)^2}{Z_t\alpha} .$$

Thus,

$$d = \frac{\partial \ln L}{\partial \alpha} = - \frac{1}{2} \Sigma \frac{Z_t'}{Z_t\alpha} - \frac{1}{2} \Sigma \frac{Z_t'\varepsilon_t^2}{(Z_t\alpha)^2} ,$$

which equals under H_o:

$$- \frac{1}{2\sigma^2} \Sigma Z_t' + \frac{1}{2\sigma^4} \Sigma Z_t' \varepsilon_t^2$$

$$= \frac{1}{2} \Sigma \frac{Z_t'}{\sigma^2} (\frac{\varepsilon_t^2}{\sigma^2} -1).$$

It should also be noted that:

$$\frac{\partial \ln L}{\partial \beta} = \Sigma \frac{\varepsilon_t X_t'}{Z_t\alpha}$$

$$= \frac{1}{\sigma^2} \Sigma \varepsilon_t X_t' \quad \text{under } H_o.$$

To obtain the information matrix under the null, we can proceed immediately to take second derivatives:

$$\frac{\partial^2 \ln L}{\partial\alpha\partial\alpha'} = \frac{\partial}{\partial\alpha}\left[\frac{1}{2}\Sigma \frac{Z_t'}{Z_t\alpha}\left(\frac{\varepsilon_t^2}{Z_t\alpha} - 1\right)\right]$$

$$= \Sigma\left(-\frac{1}{2}\right)\frac{Z_t' Z_t}{(Z_t\alpha)^2}\left(\frac{\varepsilon_t^2}{Z_t\alpha} - 1\right) + \Sigma\left(-\frac{1}{2}\right)\frac{Z_t'}{Z_t\alpha}\frac{\varepsilon_t^2 Z_t}{(Z_t\alpha)^2} .$$

Taking expectations under the null we have:

$$= -\frac{1}{2}\Sigma\frac{Z_t' Z_t \sigma^2}{\sigma^6}$$

$$= -\frac{1}{2}\Sigma\frac{Z_t' Z_t}{\sigma^4} .$$

Negating, this equals $\frac{1}{2}\Sigma\frac{Z_t' Z_t}{\sigma^4} = \frac{1}{2\sigma^4} Z' Z$, where Z is the matrix whose t^{th} row is Z_t. Similarly,

$$\frac{\partial^2 \ln L}{\partial\beta\partial\beta'} = \frac{\partial}{\partial\beta}\left(\Sigma \frac{X_t'(y_t - X_t B)}{Z_t\alpha}\right)$$

$$= -\frac{\Sigma X_t' X_t}{Z_t\alpha} .$$

Taking negative expectations under the null gives:

$$\Sigma\frac{X_t' X_t}{\sigma^2} = \frac{1}{\sigma^2}(X' X) .$$

In addition,

$$\frac{\partial^2 \ln L}{\partial\alpha\ \partial\beta} = \frac{\partial}{\partial\alpha}\left(\Sigma\frac{X_t' \varepsilon_t}{Z_t\ \alpha}\right)$$

$$= -\Sigma\frac{X_t' \varepsilon_t Z_t}{(Z_t\alpha)^2}$$

= 0, after taking negative expectations under the null.

Thus,

$$I / H_o = \begin{bmatrix} (X'X/\sigma^2) & \cdots & 0 \\ (K \times K) & & (K \times (p+1)) \\ \vdots & & \vdots \\ 0 & \cdots & (Z'Z/(2\sigma^4)) \\ ((p+1) \times K) & & ((p+1) \times (p+1)) \end{bmatrix}$$

and $I^{\alpha\alpha}/H_o = 2\sigma^4(Z'\ Z)^{-1}$.

Now we can construct the LM statistic as:

$$LM = (\frac{1}{2\sigma^2} Z'f)'(2\sigma^4(Z'\ Z)^{-1})(\frac{1}{2\sigma^2} Z'f)$$

$$= \frac{1}{2} f'\ Z(Z'\ Z)^{-1}Z'f$$

where $f_t = (\frac{\varepsilon_t^2}{\sigma^2} - 1)$ and $f = [f_t]$, a (T x 1) vector.

This test shares the optimality property of maximum local power with the likelihood-ratio and Wald tests. (See, for example, Engle (1982a).) In addition, the LM statistic may be calculated by regressing the squared residuals (from a regression of y on X) on an intercept and p own lags. TR^2 from such a regression is then asymptotically equivalent to LM, and Diebold and Pauly (1985) show that the power characteristics of the two versions of the test are essentially identical for sample sizes greater than 150, both for first order ARCH processes and higher order processes.

Once the LM test has determined that ARCH effects are operative, maximum-likelihood estimation should be undertaken. Engle (1982b) has shown that the efficiency of MLE relative to LS is very large, and may approach infinity. Due to the block diagonality of the information matrix, the MLE's may be calculated by the method of scoring, which involves an iterative sequence of LS regressions on transformed variables. This is rather tedious, however, relative to straightforward numerical maximization of the log likelihood, which is directly applicable in both the univariate and multivariate cases. For this reason full maximum-likelihood estimation is used throughout this book.

2.5) The Asymptotic Distributions of Some Common Serial Correlation Test Statistics in the Presence of ARCH

2.5.1) Background

The problem of testing for serial correlation arises constantly in time-series econometrics. Sometimes, as with forward premia in efficient markets studies, the time series to be tested for serial correlation is directly observed. Sometimes, as with residuals from an estimated model, the observed series is only an estimate of the true, but unknown, series to be tested for serial correlation. Either way, the presence of heteroskedasticity violates the assumptions upon which tests for serial correlation rest.

This observation is particularly crucial in light of the recent realization that conditional heteroskedasticity may be commonly present in the time-series context. (See, for example, Engle (1982b), Weiss (1984), Domowitz and Hakkio (1985), Diebold and Pauly (1986), and Tsay (1987), inter alia.) There are two approaches to resolution of the problem. First, one may attempt to develop tests for serial correlation that are robust to heteroskedasticty of unknown form. This is the approach taken by Domowitz and Hakkio (1983) who combine Godfrey's (1978) Lagrange multiplier test for serial correlation with White's (1980) heteroskedasticity-consistent covariance matrix estimator. The advantage of such an approach is its generality; the cost is reduced power in situations when the form of the heteroskedasticity is known or can be well approximated.

The second approach is to parameterize, or approximate, the form of the heteroskedasticity, and develop serial correlation tests specifically taking it into account. This of course has costs and benefits opposite those of the Domowitz-Hakkio approach. To the extent that the heteroskedasticity approximation is accurate, the test will perform well, and vice versa.

The model of autoregressive conditional heteroskedasticty (ARCH) due to Engle (1982b) has been found to provide a parsimonious and descriptively accurate approximation in many contexts (inflation: Engle (1982c), foreign exchange markets: Domowitz and Hakkio (1985), Diebold and Pauly (1986), Diebold and Nerlove (1986); stock market: Diebold, Lee and Im (1985); term structure of interest rates: Engle, Lillien and Robbins (1987)). In this section we consider the properties of two important model specification tools, the sample autocorrelation function and the Box-Pierce (1970) and Ljung-Box (1978) "portmanteau" statistics, in the presence of ARCH. The theory of the Bartlett standard errors is first developed, and then the portmanteau tests are treated. We build upon the results if Milhoj (1985) to show why the presence of ARCH renders the usual Bartlett standard error bands overly conservative, relative to the nominal 5% test size, and we develop an ARCH-corrected standard error estimate. This leads directly to ARCH-corrected confidence intervals under the null of uncorrelated white noise. We then treat the Box-Pierce and Box-Ljung serial correlation test statistics and show that they do not have the usual χ^2 limiting null distribution. An appropriate normalization is found which does have a limiting χ^2 distribution, however. The results are illustrated with a numerical example.

2.5.2) Correcting the Bartlett Standard Error Bands

Consider a zero-mean time series $\{x_t\}_{t=1}^{T}$. It can be shown (Anderson (1942), Bartlett (1946)) that, under the null of Gaussian white noise, the sample autocorrelation at lag τ :

$$\hat{\rho}(\tau) = \frac{\hat{\gamma}(\tau)}{\hat{\gamma}(0)} \quad ,$$

where $\hat{\gamma}(\tau) = 1/T \, \Sigma \, x_t \, x_{t-\tau}$ is asymptotically normally distributed with mean 0 and variance:

$$\mathrm{var}\ (\hat{\rho}(\tau)) = \frac{T - \tau}{T\ (T + 2)} ,$$

or, as a further approximation, 1/T. This result leads to the so-called Bartlett 95% confidence interval under the null:

$$\rho(\tau) = 0.0 \pm \frac{1.96}{\sqrt{T}} .$$

Under ARCH, however, the sample autocorrelations are normal with mean 0 and variance:

$$(1/T)\ (1 + \frac{\gamma_{x^2}(\tau)}{\sigma^4})$$

where $\gamma_{x^2}(\tau)$ is the autocovariance at lag τ for the squared process $\{x_t^2\}_{t=1}^{T}$ and σ^4 is the squared unconditional variance of the x process. (See Milhoj (1985).) Because:

$$\frac{\gamma_{x^2}(\tau)}{\sigma^4} > 0 \quad \text{for all } \tau$$

it is clear that Bartlett's standard error is "too small" in the presence of ARCH, in the sense that, for example, the <u>true</u> 95% confidence interval is wider than the <u>computed</u> "95%" confidence interval. Note, however, that:

$$\lim_{\tau \to \infty} \quad (1/T)\ (\ 1 + \frac{\gamma_{x^2}(\tau)}{\sigma^4}\ ) = 1/T$$

since $\gamma_{x^2}(\tau) \to 0$ as $\tau \to \infty$, by stationarity and ergodicity of $\{x^2\}$. Because $\gamma_{x^2}(\tau)$ and σ^2 are easily consistently estimated, we can construct a consistent estimate of the variance of the sample autocorrelations as:

$$S(\tau) = (1/T)\ (1 + \frac{\hat{\gamma}_{x^2}(\tau)}{\hat{\sigma}^4})$$

which leads to the corrected confidence interval:

$$\rho_x(\tau) = 0.0 \pm 1.96 \left(S(\tau)\right)^{1/2} .$$

To implement the results over, say, the first K autocorrelations, we first obtain:

$$\hat{\rho}_x(\tau) = \frac{\Sigma x_t x_{t-\tau}}{\Sigma x_t^2}, \quad \tau = 1 \ldots K$$

$$\hat{\sigma}^4 = (\hat{\sigma}^2)^2 = (1/T \; \Sigma \; x_t^2)^2$$

$$\hat{\gamma}_{x^2}(\tau) = 1/T \; \Sigma \; (x_t^2 - \hat{\sigma}^2)\,(x_{t-\tau}^2 - \hat{\sigma}^2), \quad \tau = 1 \ldots K$$

and then construct the bands via the above formula.

To illustrate, 500 observations are generated on the process:

$$x_t = \varepsilon_t, \quad \varepsilon_t \mid \varepsilon_{t-1} \sim N(0, \sigma_t^2), \quad \sigma_t^2 = \alpha_0 + \alpha_1 \varepsilon_{t-1}^2 .$$

The first 20 autocorrelations of x are calculated, along with the Bartlett 1.96 standard error bands and the ARCH-corrected Bartlett 1.96 standard error bands. One thousand replications are performed for each of ten points in the parameter space: $\alpha_1 = 0.0, .1, .2, .3, .4, .5, .6, .7, .8, .9$. Without loss of generality, we can set $\alpha_0 = 1 - \alpha_1$ (Pantula (1985)), which maintains the unconditional variance at 1.0. The case of $\alpha_1 = 0.0$ of course corresponds to independent white noise. The realizations are generated via the cannonical form:

$$\varepsilon_t = N_t(0,1)(\alpha_0 + \alpha_1 \varepsilon_{t-1}^2)^{1/2}$$

where we set $\varepsilon_0 = 0$. The same one-thousand sets of 500 innovations $\{N_t(0,1)\}_{t=1}^{500}$ were used to generate the ARCH realization at each explored point of the sample space; this provides powerful variance reduction. The proportions of rejections (in 1000 repetitions over 20 autocorrelations) relative to the uncorrected Bartlett 95% confidence interval are given in Table 2.1 as P, while rejection frequencies relative to the corrected intervals appear as P_c.

The results are easily interpreted. When $\alpha_1 = 0$, of course, the nominal size (5%) approximately equals the actual size (4.6%). This is also true if the ARCH correction is (needlessly) applied. As α_1 rises, however, so too does the empirical size of the uncorrected confidence interval, so that, for example, when $\alpha_1 = .9$, the probability of a type I error is more than twice the nominal probability of 5%. The ARCH-corrected intervals, on the other hand, maintain nominal size.

The problem of spurious "significance" of sample autocorrelations due to ARCH becomes progressively less serious for progressively higher-ordered autocorrelations, due to the earlier mentioned fact that the "correction factor" tends to unity as $\tau \to \infty$. This is of little value in practice, however, because it is precisely the low-order autocorrelations which are typically calculated. The calculation of twenty sample autocorrelations in the simulations reported above was done with the eventual calculation of Box-Pierce statistics in mind; had fewer sample autocorrelations been calculated, the average deviation from nominal test size would have been substantially larger.

Consider, for example, the ARCH(1) case described above. The reader may verify that:

$$\frac{\gamma_{x^2}(\tau)}{\sigma^4} = \frac{2\alpha_1^\tau}{1-3\,\alpha_1^2},$$

so that the standard error is:

$$\frac{1}{\sqrt{T}}\left(1 + \frac{2\,\alpha_1^\tau}{1-3\,\alpha_1^2}\right)^{1/2}.$$

The corrected and uncorrected confidence intervals are shown in Figure 2.2 for $\alpha_1 = .5$. Clearly, most of the divergence occurs at the low-order autocorrelations. The deviation from nominal test size is different at each autocorrelation lag, becoming progressively smaller as the lag order gets larger. Thus, to repeat for emphasis, the entries in the first row of Table 2.1 are very conservative, in the sense that it is not uncommon practice to examine only the first 5 or 10 autocorrelations, which would lead to much higher rejection proportions. This is strongly illustrated in the first row of Table 2.2, which reports rejection proportions based on only the first 5 sample autocorrelations.

It is of interest to note that the probabilities of type I error may be calculated analytically, as follows. Under the Bartlett assumption of true independent, identically distributed noise,

$$\hat{\rho}_x(\tau) \overset{a}{\sim} N\left(0, \frac{1}{T}\right) = N\left((0, C_1(T)\right) .$$

In reality, however,

$$\hat{\rho}_x(\tau) \overset{a}{\sim} N\left(0, \frac{1}{T}\left(\frac{2\,\alpha_1^{\tau}}{1-3\,\alpha_1^2}\right)\right) = N\left(0, C_2(T,\tau)\right) .$$

Thus, the probability that $\hat{\rho}_x(\tau)$ exceeds 1.96 Bartlett standard errors of zero is:

$$P\left(|\hat{\rho}_x(\tau)| > 1.96\sqrt{C_1(T)}\right)$$

$$= P\left[\left(|\hat{\rho}_x(\tau)| / \sqrt{C_2(T,\tau)}\right) > 1.96\,\frac{\sqrt{C_1(T)}}{\sqrt{C_2(T,\tau)}}\right]$$

$$= P\left(|Z| > 1.96\,\frac{\sqrt{C_1(T)}}{\sqrt{C_2(T,\tau)}}\right)$$

where Z is a N(0,1) random variable. Since $[C_1(T) / C_2(T,\tau)] < 1$, for all T, τ, it follows that $P(\cdot) > .05$. If $\alpha_1 = .5$ and $T = 500$, for example, the probabilities of type I error are $.378(\tau = 1)$, $.164(\tau = 3)$, $.100(\tau = 5)$, and $.051(\tau = 10)$.

2.5.3) On the Existence of EX_t^4

Strictly speaking, the above results require existence of the fourth raw moment of x, μ_4. This is because:

$$\gamma_{x^2}(\tau) = \alpha_1 \gamma_{x^2}(\tau-1) + \dots + \alpha_p \gamma_{x^2}(\tau-p)$$

with

$$\gamma_{x^2}(0) = EX_t^4 - \sigma^4$$
$$= \mu_4 - \sigma^4.$$

Thus, if μ_4 does not exist (i.e., is infinite) then neither does $\gamma_{x^2}(\tau)$. Milhoj (1985) shows that a necessary and sufficient condition for existence of μ_4 for a pth-order ARCH process is given by:

$$3\ \alpha' \ (I-\Psi)^{-1} \alpha < 1$$

where $\alpha' = (\alpha_1, \dots, \alpha_p)$ and $\underset{(p\times p)}{\Psi}$ is defined by $\Psi_{ij} = \alpha_{i+j} + \alpha_{i-j}$,

where we set $\alpha_k = 0$ for $k \leq 0$ and $k > p$.

In actual applications, of course, it is not known whether the condition is satisfied, and the analyst should proceed under the assumption that it is. Even if the true moment of interest has infinite value, the best sample approximation for the purposes of correcting the Bartlett standard errors will still be obtained by following the procedure outlined above.

As an example, consider again the ARCH(1) case. Then the existence condition for μ_4 boils down to:

$$\alpha_1 < 1/\sqrt{3} = .577.$$

Thus, in the earlier-tabulated example, the cases of $\alpha_1 = .6, .7, .8,$ and $.9$ all correspond to $\mu_4 = \infty$, yet the ARCH correction continues to work well.

2.5.4) The Box-Pierce and Ljung-Box Statistics

The Box-Pierce (1970) serial correlation test statistic (to lag K) is given by:

$$BP(K) = T \sum_{\tau=1}^{K} \hat{\rho}_x^2(\tau).$$

Due to its direct dependence $\hat{\rho}_x^2$, it is also affected by ARCH and must be modified if nominal size is to be maintained. Since under the null of independent white noise we know that:

$$\hat{\rho}(\tau) \xrightarrow{d} N(0,1/T), \quad \tau = 1, 2, 3, \ldots,$$

we have:

$$\sqrt{T}\, \hat{\rho}(\tau) \xrightarrow{d} N(0,1).$$

Thus,

$$T \hat{\rho}^2(\tau) \xrightarrow{d} \chi_1^2$$

and therefore by asymptotic independence of the sample autocorrelations:

$T \sum_{\tau=1}^{K} \hat{\rho}^2(\tau) \xrightarrow{d} \chi_K^2$, which is the Box-Pierce result.

Under ARCH, however,

$$\rho(\tau) \xrightarrow{d} N\left(0, 1/T\left(1 + \frac{\gamma_{x^2}(\tau)}{\sigma^4}\right)\right).$$

Thus,

$$\left\{T \Big/ \left(1 + \frac{\gamma_{x^2}(\tau)}{\sigma^4}\right)\right\}^{1/2} \hat{\rho}_x(\tau) \xrightarrow{d} N(0,1),$$

so:

$$\left\{T \Big/ \left(1 + \frac{\gamma_{x^2}(\tau)}{\sigma^4}\right)\right\} \hat{\rho}_x^2(\tau) \xrightarrow{d} \chi_1^2$$

and:

$$T \sum_{\tau=1}^{K} \left[\frac{\sigma^4}{\sigma^4 + \gamma_{x^2}(\tau)}\right] \hat{\rho}_\tau^2 \overset{a}{\sim} \chi_K^2.$$

Because the bracketed term is less than or equal to one for all τ, each term in the sum involved in the uncorrected Box-Pierce statistic is "too large," leading to larger than nominal size.

The empirical sizes of the standard and corrected Box-Pierce statistics are shown below in Table 2.1 (K = 20) and Table 2.2 (K = 5); the ARCH-corrected statistics perform quite well. It is interesting to note that the very large deviations from nominal size (i.e., much larger than the average deviation of the first 20 sample autocorrelations reported earlier) of the uncorrected Box-Pierce statistics in the presence of ARCH are due to the "cumulation" of errors. This is true regardless of the value of K. Of course, as argued earlier, the problem is made worse as K decreases; this is easily seen by comparing the third rows of Tables 2.1 and 2.2.

Similarly, the Ljung-Box (1978) statistic:

$$LB(K) = T\,(T+2)\sum_{\tau=1}^{K}(T-\tau)^{-1}\rho_x^2(\tau),$$

of which the Box-Pierce statistic is an asymptotic approximation, may be easily corrected for ARCH.

2.5.5) Conclusions

In summary, we have shown that the presence of ARCH invalidates the asymptotic distributions of the sample autocorrelations and the Box-Pierce and Box-Ljung test statistics for serial correlation, when computed in the usual fashion. It was shown, both analytically and numerically, that the presence of ARCH renders empirical size (i.e., probability of Type I error) larger than nominal size, leading to spuriously "significant" sample autocorrelations and portmanteau diagnostics. Appropriate correction factors were developed and shown to produce highly satisfactory results, with nominal and empirical sizes being approximately equal.

We have also shown that the error in the Box-Pierce and Box-Ljung statistics, calculated through lag K, is progressively more severe for progressively smaller K.

This provides yet another reason, in addition to those given in Box and Pierce (p. 1513) to be wary of test statistics based on small K.

The analysis in the text focused on the case of observed time series. As is well known (Durbin (1970)), the results do not generalize directly to the case of testing for serial correlation in the residuals of estimated models, because the residual autocorrelations are approximately representable as a singular linear transformation of the true disturbance autocorrelations. Box and Pierce (1970) have, however, shown that the dimension of the singularity is equal to d, the degrees of freedom lost in estimating d model parameters. The results remain valid, then, when the statistics are tested against a χ^2_{k-d} distribution.

Finally, it should be pointed out that the presence of ARCH makes the Bartlett standard errors and the portmanteau tests more conservative; thus, a failure to reject the null of no serial correlation using the uncorrected statistics may be trusted. If the null is rejected, however, and conditional heteroskedasticity of the autoregressive type is suspected, the corrections should be employed.

2.6) Concluding Remarks

In this chapter we introduced a model of autoregressive conditional heteroskedasticity (ARCH) which will play a key role in later chapters. We showed that ARCH effects, if present, lead to clustering of prediction error variances; in particular, the conditional variance may be forecasted. The moment structure was studied in detail, and it was shown that all ARCH processes are leptokurtic, and that this leptokurtosis is reduced by temporal aggregation. We discussed that maximum likelihood parameter estimation and showed that the LM principle produces convenient hypothesis tests. Finally, well-performing ARCH-corrections for serial correlation tests were developed and illustrated.

Table 2.1
Empirical Size Results, Box-Pierce Tests
And Bartlett Standard Errors, Based on First 20 Autocorrelations*

α_1=	0	.1	.2	.3	.4	.5	.6	.7	.8	.9
P	.047	.048	.051	.057	.058	.059	.074	.084	.096	.106
Pc	.048	.048	.048	.051	.046	.046	.049	.048	.047	.044
BP	.053	.052	.063	.074	.095	.127	.215	.280	.378	.429
BPc	.052	.052	.054	.054	.044	.042	.051	.060	.063	.055

* Based on 1000 repetitions

P = Rejection Percentage, Bartlett Standard Errors
Pc = Rejection Percentage, ARCH-Corrected Bartlett Standard Errors
BP = Rejection Percentage, Box-Pierce Statistic
BPc = Rejection Percentage, ARCH-Corrected Box-Pierce Statistic

Table 2.2
Empirical Size Results, Box-Pierce Test
And Bartlett Standard Errors, Based on First 5 Autocorrelations*

α_1=	0	.1	.2	.3	.4	.5	.6	.7	.8	.9
P	.047	.062	.065	.076	.085	.113	.147	.178	.246	.285
Pc	.049	.054	.051	.048	.046	.050	.046	.042	.049	.047
BP	.049	.066	.074	.112	.151	.213	.299	.366	.523	.610
BPc	.048	.047	.048	.040	.041	.048	.047	.040	.052	.047

* Based on 1000 repetitions

P = Rejection Percentage, Bartlett Standard Errors
Pc = Rejection Percentage, ARCH-Corrected Bartlett Standard Errors
BP = Rejection Percentage, Box-Pierce Statistic
BPc = Rejection Percentage, ARCH-Corrected Box-Pierce Statistic

Figure 2.1

KURTOSIS VERSUS M

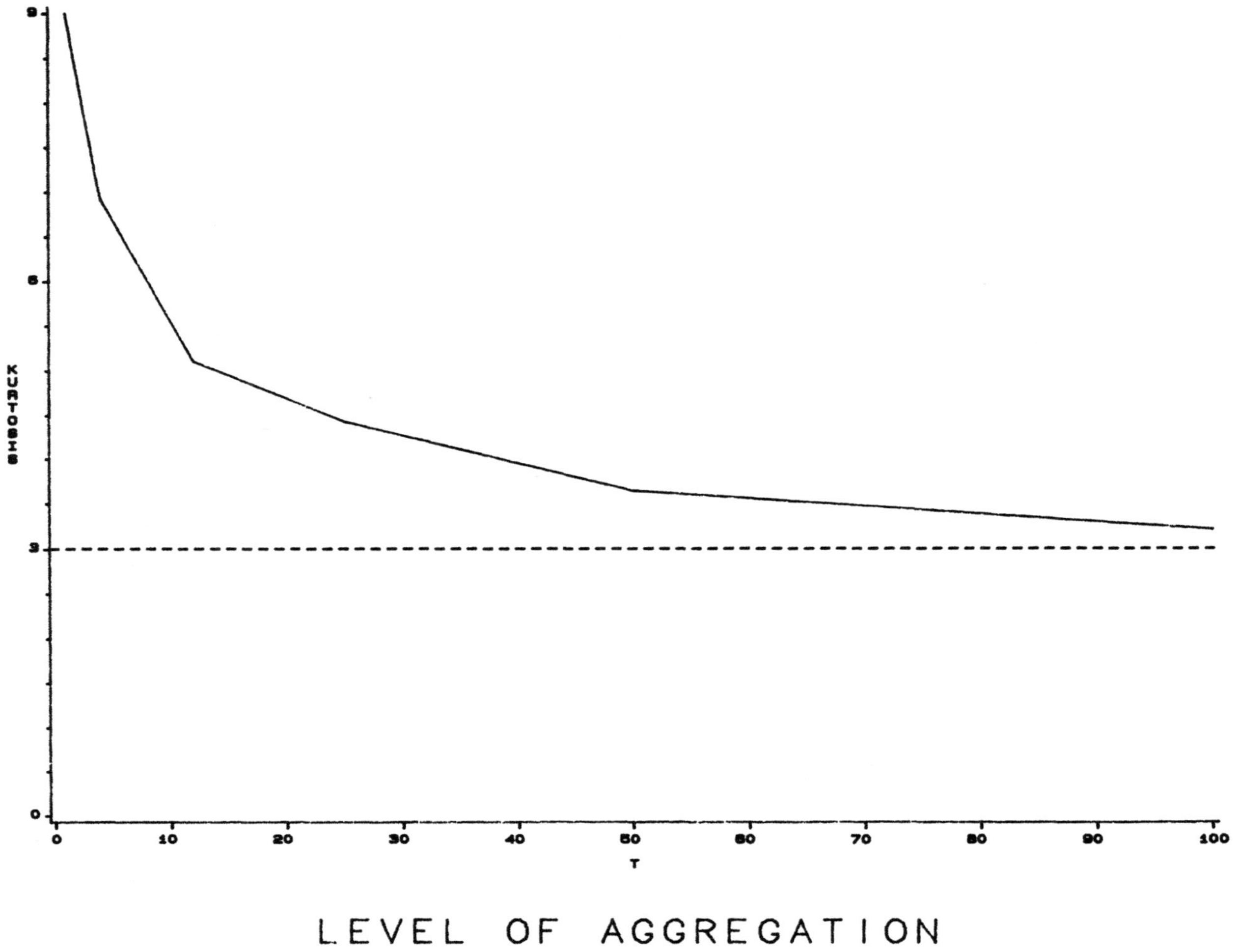

Figure 2.2

2-SIGMA INTERVALS, CORRECTED AND UNCORRECTED

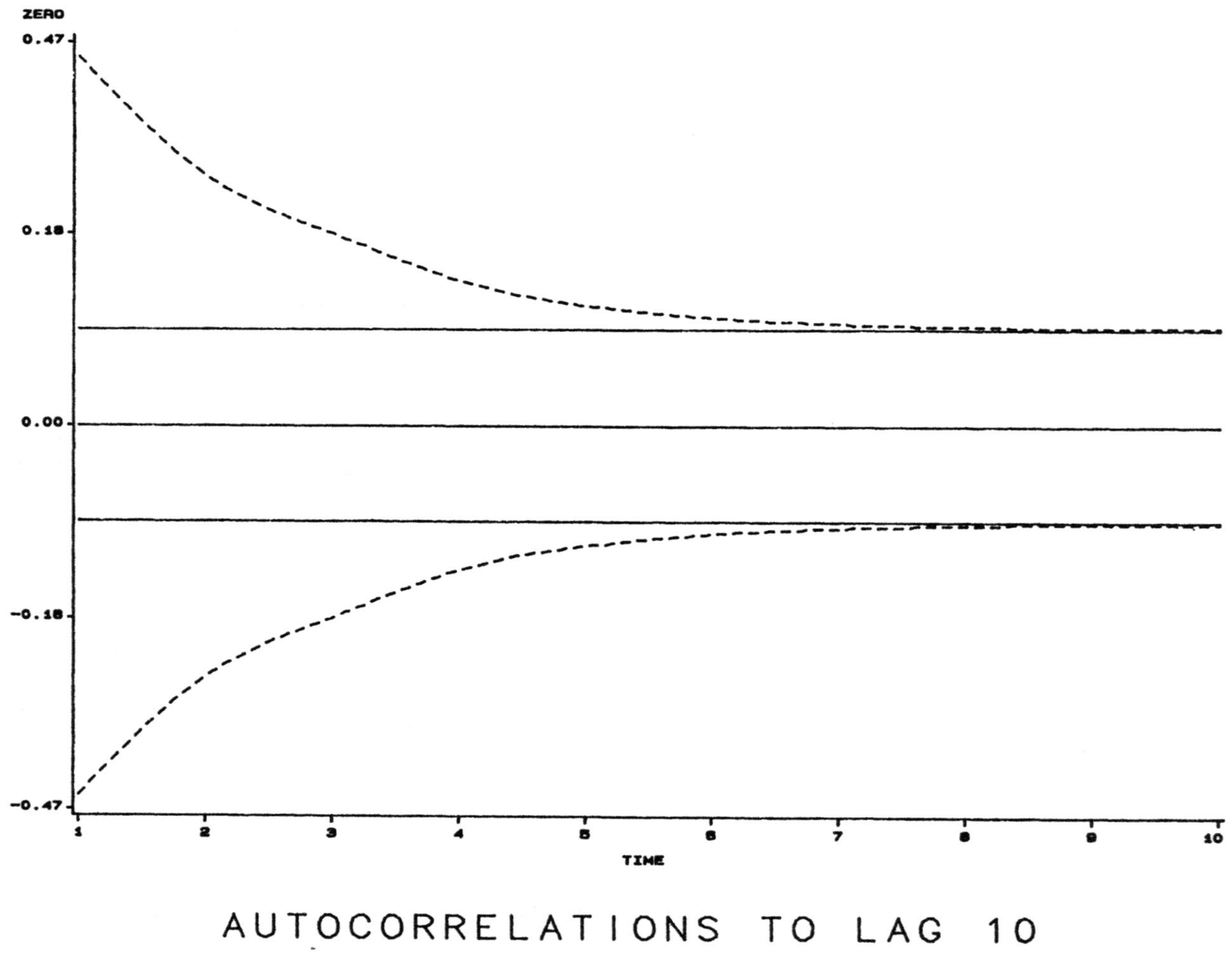

Chapter Three: Weekly Univariate Nominal Exchange Rate Fluctuations

3.1) Introduction

The difficulties involved in explaining exchange rate movements during the post-1973 float with standard purchasing power parity, monetary, or portfolio balance models have become increasingly apparent. Meese and Rogoff (1983a, 1983b) systematically document the pervasive out-of-sample empirical failure of these models, and they find that a simple random walk model predicts the major rates during the floating period as well as (or better than) any of the alternative models.[1] These models (both structural and nonstructural) include a flexible price monetary model (Frenkel, 1976; Bilson, 1979), a sticky price monetary model (Dornbusch, 1976; Frankel, 1979), a sticky price monetary model with current account effects (Hooper and Morton, 1982), six univariate time series models, a vector autoregressive model, and the forward rate.[2] The failure of the structural models is all the more striking in light of the fact that the Meese-Rogoff predictive comparisons use ex post realizations of exogenous variables.

Assertions that dollar spot rates under the recent float have followed approximate random walks are common, but formal empirical analysis of the time series properties of exchange rates is lacking in the literature.[3] In this chapter we attempt to shed light on these issues by using a number of time series techniques to study the stochastic structure of the seven major dollar spot rates: the Canadian Dollar (CD), the French Franc (FF), the Deutschemark (DM), the Italian Lira (LIR), the Japanese Yen (YEN), the Swiss Franc (SF), and the British Pound (BP). We find that, in the class of linear time series models with white noise innovations, the random walk is a very good approximation to the underlying probability structure; clearly, then, we would not

---

1 See also Meese and Rogoff (1983b), Cornell (1977), Mussa (1979), and Frenkel (1981).

2 They also investigated a variety of prefiltering and specification techniques, including the T/lnT rule (Hannan, 1970), the Akaike (1974) information criterion, the Schwarz (1978) information criterion, weighted autoregressions, and frequency domain methods.

3 For work related to the random-walk hypothesis see Meese and Singleton (1982) and Callen, Kwan, and Yip (1985). See also the related early work of Poole (1966, 1967) concerning the 1950-1962 Canadian float.

expect any other linear model to dominate in terms of predictive performance. However, when the class of models under consideration is broadened to allow for possible nonlinearities, we find strong evidence of autoregressive conditional heteroskedasticity (Engle, 1982b) in the one step ahead prediction errors, so that the disturbances in the "random walk" are uncorrelated but not independent.

The finding of autoregressive conditional heteroskedasticity (ARCH) in all of the exchange rates studied is very important. First, ARCH provides a way of formalizing the observation that large changes tend to be followed by large changes (of either sign), and small by small, leading to contiguous periods of volatility and stability. We show later that even a visual inspection of the data indicates ARCH phenomena, and the formal hypothesis testing and estimation procedures which are used enable a rigorous formulation. Second, the observed ARCH effects are consistent with the leptokurtosis in exchange rate changes, which has been well documented by Westerfield (1977) and which all of the series display; this is because ARCH processes possess "fat-tailed" unconditional densities, even though their conditional densities are normal. Thus, the results indicate that an appropriate and descriptively accurate stochastic generating process for the logarithm of spot rates is the random walk with ARCH innovations.

Another substantive result of this study is the formulation of statistically and economically meaningful measures of exchange rate volatility. The nature, time pattern, and economic effects of exchange rate volatility are recurrent topics in the literature. Volatility of exchange rates is of importance because of the uncertainty it creates for prices of exports and imports, for the value of international reserves and for open positions in foreign currency,[4] as well as for the domestic currency value of debt payments and workers' remittances, which in turn affect domestic wages, prices, output, employment, and other variables.[5] Furthermore, the degree of exchange rate volatility affects the ability of a country simultaneously to maintain internal and external balance, and is also directly related to market efficiency. With respect to

---

4 Forward markets cannot completely eliminate the risk, because of costly coverage (i.e., the forward premium) and transaction costs.

5 See Lanyi and Suss (1982).

these matters, exchange rate volatility under fixed and floating regimes and the changes (if any) in that volatility over time have been widely debated. Issues such as the relationship of Federal Reserve operating procedures to exchange rate volatility, the effects of exchange rate volatility on the natural rate of unemployment, the effects of volatility on the bid/ask spread as well as on the volume and prices of internationally traded goods, and so on, have received attention.[6] Furthermore, under risk aversion, risk premia will form a "wedge" in international equilibrium conditions such as uncovered interest parity and may therefore influence the determination of spot exchange rates. Risk premia depend on the variability of the distribution of future spot rates, which (as shown below) is nonconstant. The resulting time-varying risk premia have been studied by Domowitz and Hakkio (1985) and Diebold and Pauly (1987).

A generally acceptable measure of volatility has not been found, however, although several have been proposed. Moving variances, moving average absolute deviations, as well as standard error of moving trend regressions and moving autoregressions, have been tried, but for reasons discussed below none is really satisfactory. Moreover, the many different measures which have been used often make potentially complementary studies incomparable.[7]

First, the "moving sample" approach to volatility calculation can lead to seriously misleading results. The implicit assumption is that volatility changes over time, and the use of a moving sample represents a crude attempt to capture those changes. However, if volatility is changing over time, then the moving sample approach is always suboptimal because it throws away information; rather, some attempt should be made to uncover and model the nature of the time-varying volatility. On the other hand, if the volatility is not time varying, then the moving sample approach will

---

6 See, for example, Bergstrand (1983), Zis (1983), Akhtar and Hilton (1984), Levich (1985), Kennen and Rodrick (1985), Huang (1981), Frenkel and Mussa (1983), Hooper and Kohlhagen (1978), Kreinin (1977), and Cushman (1983). To place the work in historical perspective, see also the seminal papers by Friedman (1953) and Johnson (1969).

7 See, for example, Kennen and Rodrick (1985). By "moving" volatility measures, we mean that they are calculated on a moving subset of available data, such as the most recent v observations. The most common example is a movong variance about a moving mean.

produce volatility measures that nevertheless appear time varying, sometimes strongly so. Second, volatility measures not based on sample second moments are inconsistent with mean-variance expected utility analysis. Thus, for example, measures based on average absolute deviations are of limited value. Finally, the conditional, rather than the unconditional, second moment should be the focus when studying volatility, since any uncertainty in exchange rate movements which can be removed by conditioning upon other variables or upon the past is economically irrelevant. In this respect, the use of the standard error of moving trend regressions or autoregressions is appropriate, but the approach remains subject to the same criticisms regarding moving samples.

The problem, of course, is that standard tests and models of unconditional heteroskedasticity are irrelevant, while tests for conditional heteroskedasticity are difficult to apply, because they require knowledge of the "forcing variables" which drive the variance. ARCH models, on the other hand, provide a parsimonious and accurate description of an evolving conditional variance. We may view the ARCH model as using a set of latent variables (past squared innovations) to drive the conditional variance. By estimating an appropriate ARCH model for each exchange rate, we can solve for the implied time series of conditional variances, and thus obtain a meaningful measure of volatility for that rate.

Finally, our finding of random walks with ARCH disturbances means that, although $\Delta \ln S_t$ cannot be forecast, its changing variance can be forecast.[8] Thus, ARCH may be exploited to obtain time-varying confidence intervals for point forecasts of exchange rate changes (zero for a random-walk model). In periods of high volatility these intervals are large, and in less volatile periods they are smaller. This stands in marked contrast to the standard constant variance random-walk model, which ignores the changing environment in which forecasts are produced and the associated temporal movements in forecast error variances.

[8] Here and throughout, $\ln S_t$ is a generic expression standing for any or all of the log exchange rate series.

3.2) Moving Sample Moments as Volatility Measures

Before proceeding further, we pause to illustrate the misleading results that can arise when moving sample moments are used as volatility measures. Consider the time series $y_t \sim N(0, \sigma^2)$. In this case, the conditional variance, which happens to be equal to the unconditional variance, is not time-varying. A researcher looking at the data, however, has no immediate way of knowing that fact and so we consider the properties of the usual moving variance calculated about a moving mean. The N-period moving variance is given by:

$$\bar{S}_t = (1 / N+1) \sum_{i=0}^{N} (y_{t-i} - \bar{y}_t)^2$$

where $\bar{y}_t$ is the N-period moving mean given by:

$$\bar{y}_t = (1 / N+1) \sum_{i=0}^{N} y_{t-i} .$$

We can rewrite this as:

$$\bar{S}_t = (1 / N+1) \sum_{i=0}^{N} (y_{t-i}^2 + \bar{y}_t^2 - 2\bar{y}_t y_{t-i})$$

$$= (1 / N+1) \sum_{i=0}^{N} y_{y-i}^2 + \bar{y}_t^2 - 2\bar{y}_t (1 / N+1) \sum_{i=0}^{N} y_{t-i}$$

$$=(1 / N+1) \sum_{i=0}^{N} y_{t-i}^2 - \bar{y}_t^2 .$$

If we let $\{N_t(0, 1)\}$ be an iid sequence of Gaussian random variables with mean zero and variance one such that $y_t = \sigma N_t$, then:

$$\bar{S}_t = (1 / N+1) \sum_{i=0}^{N} (\sigma N_{t-i})^2 - \bar{y}_t^2$$

$$= (\sigma^2 / N+1) \sum_{i=0}^{N} \chi_{1,t-i}^2 - \bar{y}_t^2$$

where $\chi^2_{1,t}$ is a time-t realization of a chi-square random variable with one degree of freedom such that $\chi^2_{1,t} = N^2_t$. Because we want to study the time-series properties of $\{\bar{S}_t\}$, it will prove useful to adopt the normalization:

$$\bar{S}'_t = (N+1 / \sigma^2)\ \bar{S}_t \ .$$

Then,

$$\bar{S}'_t = \underbrace{\sum_{i=0}^{N} \chi^2_{1,t-i}}_{A} - \underbrace{\bar{y}^2_t\ (N+1 / \sigma^2)}_{B} \ .$$

Part A of this expression is an N-period moving-average process whose innovations follow a chi-square distribution with one degree of freedom. Furthermore, it is noninvertible for all N, and therefore displays substantial persistence. This is one source of the spurious temporal movements in $\bar{S}'_t$. The other source is the term denoted by B, which is particularly interesting because of the nonlinearities introduced through $\bar{y}^2_t$. For example, consider the first-order case N = 1. Then:

$$\bar{S}_t = 1/2\ y^2_t + 1/2\ y^2_{t-1} - \bar{y}^2_t$$

$$= \sigma^2/2\ \chi^2_{1,t} + \sigma^2/2\ \chi^2_{1,t-1} - \bar{y}^2_t$$

$$= \sigma^2/2\ \chi^2_{1,t} + \sigma^2/2\ \chi^2_{1,t-1} - 1/4\ y^2_t - 1/4\ y^2_{t-1} - 1/2\ y_t y_{t-1}$$

$$= \sigma^2/2\ \chi^2_{1,t} + \sigma^2/2\ \chi^2_{1,t-1} - 1/4\ (\sigma N_t)^2 - 1/4\ (\sigma N_{t-1})^2 - 1/2\ (\sigma^2 N_t N_{t-1})$$

$$= \sigma^2/2\ \chi^2_{1,t} + \sigma^2/2\ \chi^2_{1,t-1} - \sigma^2/4\ \chi^2_{1,t} - \sigma^2/4\ \chi^2_{1,t-1} - \sigma^2/2\ N_t N_{t-1}$$

$$= \sigma^2/4\ \chi^2_{1,t} + \sigma^2/4\ \chi^2_{1,t-1} - \sigma^2/2\ N_t N_{t-1} \ .$$

The nonlinearity is clearly evident in the $N_t N_{t-1}$ term.

To highlight these effects, we generate 100 pseudorandom normal deviates with zero mean and unit variance using IMSL subroutine GGNML, and the time-series of two-period, ten-period, and twenty-five-period moving sample variances are computed. They are shown in Figures 3.1 and 3.2. While all three series are centered at unity, they display substantial time variation. As expected, the amplitude of fluctuations is higher for the two-period moving variance, while the persistence is stronger for the ten- and twenty-five-period moving variances. Either way, however, the uncritical use of moving sample moments (or residuals from moving regressions) as volatility measures may lead to severe data misinterpretation.

3.3) The Data

We study weekly spot rates from the first week of July 1973 to the second week of August 1985. All data are interbank closing spot prices (bid side), Wednesdays, taken from the International Monetary Markets Yearbook. Wednesdays were chosen because very few holidays occur on that day, and there is no problem of "weekend effects."

By "weekend effect" we do not necessarily mean a calendar effect associated with the regular occurrence of weekends, although such effects may arise as well. More generally, we are referring to the temporal line-up problem of, for example, the occurrence of weekends in a daily sample. In the AR(1) representation:

$$\ln S_t = \rho \ln S_{t-1} + \varepsilon_t ,$$

for example, we have good reason to suspect that the relationship between Monday (t) and Friday (t-1) differs from that of contiguous business days, due to the different amount of information coming to the market over the weekend.

In our sample of 632 observations, fewer than eight holidays occur on a Wednesday; when they did, the observation for the following Thursday was used. Working (1960) and Meese and Rogoff (1983a) argue that point sample data are more desirable than weekly averages, since if the true model follows a random walk on a day to day basis then the series of weekly averages exhibits positive serial correlation. Following standard convention, all exchange rates except the pound are measured in units of local currency per dollar.

All of the analysis presented below is based on the log spot rate, in order to conform with the literature and avoid some technical problems. The log specification avoids prediction problems arising from Jensen's inequality (Meese and Rogoff, 1983a) and $(1 - L)\ln S_t$ has the convenient interpretation of approximate percentage change.[9]

The data were not seasonally adjusted, due to the spurious serial correlation which filters such as X-11 can introduce. (See Grether and Nerlove (1970), Cleveland and Tiao (1976) and Nerlove, Grether and Carvalho (1979).) Instead, we chose to use time and frequency domain approaches to investigate the presence of seasonality and model it if found to occur; this is in the spirit of the new "model-based" approach to seasonal adjustment as surveyed in Bell and Hilmer (1984). Of course, temporal arbitrage makes pronounced seasonality unlikely in exchange rates, and the data show no evidence of it.

3.4) Model Formulation

Plots of the log exchange rates are given in Figures 3.3 through 3.9. The appreciation of the dollar which began in 1980 is evident in each of the exchange rates studied. Depreciation of the currency is indicated by an exchange rate increase, except for the BP, for which the opposite is true. Similarly, the beginnings of the recent decline in the dollar are evident in the last few observations of each series. The pre-1980 period, on the other hand, is characterized by less coherence in the exchange rate fluctuations, with the SF, YEN, BP and DM appreciating versus the dollar,

---

9 Jensen's inequality ensures that $E\left(\frac{1}{S}\right) \neq \frac{1}{E(S)}$, where S is the exchange rate measured in units of foreign currency per unit of local currency. Thus, for example, while the DM/$ rate is the reciprocal of the $/DM rate, their expected values are not reciprocals.

while the FF, LIR and CD either held steady or depreciated.

A visual inspection indicates nonstationarity in each of the series, although its form may not be the same for each series. For example, the DM, YEN, SF and BP display no apparent trend; instead, they appear to be homogeneous nonstationary processes, meaning that they are stationary and invertible after suitable differencing. The CD, FF, and LIR, on the other hand, have a prolonged history of depreciation versus the dollar, so that a "trend plus irregular" model might be more reasonable, where the irregular component could be either stationary or integrated. Thus, because homogeneous nonstationarity of order one implies that the local behavior of the series is invariant up to level, while homogeneous nonstationarity of order two implies invariance up to level and slope,[10] the graphs indicate that a first difference is almost certainly required to achieve stationarity, and that a second difference may be required as well. Differencing must be undertaken with caution, however, because if the true model is trend plus a stationary disturbance, then differencing will remove the trend but introduce a unit root into the moving-average component of the stationary disturbance. Trended and integrated series also have very different properties in terms of prediction, as we show below.

The sample autocorrelation functions are calculated for each series up to lag 40 and clearly indicate homogeneous nonstationarity, as evidenced by the fact that all are positive, fail to damp, and have very smooth, persistent movements.[11] Even the YEN, whose autocorrelation function declines the most quickly, has a sample autocorrelation of .848 at lag 20. The first twelve sample autocorrelations of each series are given in Table 3.1.

The sample partial autocorrelation functions are also calculated for each of the seven exchange rates, and the results are qualitatively the same for each series: each has a very large and highly significant value (extremely close to one) at lag 1, while the values at all other lags are insignificantly different from zero. Specifically, the lag 1 sample partial autocorrelations for the CD, FF, DM, LIR, YEN, SF, BP are,

---

[10] See Box and Jenkins (1976).
[11] This is conforms to the results of Wichern (1973) and Granger and Newbold (1977).

respectively, .99, 1.00, 1.00, 1.00, 1.00, 1.00 and .99. It is clear that the distinct cutoff in the sample partial autocorrelation functions after lag 1, the smooth and slowly declining behavior of the sample autocorrelation functions, and the values of the highly significant first sample partial autocorrelation strongly suggest first order homogeneous nonstationarity in general, and the random walk in particular, for each series. The first twelve sample partial autocorrelations are given in Table 3.2.

Estimation of the spectral density functions confirmed these results; each was absolutely dominated by a single large low frequency peak, sharply concentrated at the origin.[12]

To summarize, then, we have argued that each series is highly nonstationary and presented some preliminary evidence indicative of random walk, or at least homogeneous, behavior. As pointed out earlier, however, we must be wary of uncritical differencing. Four candidate models are therefore considered:

M1) lnS is stationary about a nonzero mean:

$$\Phi_1(L)\ (\ln S_t - \mu_1) = \Theta_1(L)\ \varepsilon_{1t},$$

where all roots of Φ_1, and Θ_1 are outside the unit circle.

M2) lnS is integrated of order one about a nonzero mean:

$$(1 - L)\ \Phi_2(L)\ (\ln S_t - \mu_2) = \Theta_2(L)\ \varepsilon_{2t},$$

where all roots of Φ_2 and Θ_2 are outside the unit circle.

M3) lnS has stationary deviations from linear trend:

$$\Phi_3(L)\ (\ln S_t - \beta_0^3 - \beta_1^3\ t) = \Theta_3(L)\ \varepsilon_{3t},$$

where all roots of Φ_3 and Θ_3 are outside the unit circle.

M4) lnS is integrated about a linear trend:

---

[12] The weights were 1/25 ... 7/25 ... 1/25.

$$(1 - L)\ \Phi_4(L)\ (\ln S_t - \beta_0^4 - \beta_1^4\ t) = \Theta_4(L)\ \varepsilon_{4t}, .$$

where all roots of Φ_4 and Θ_4 are outside the unit circle.

It is immediately clear that only in models M2 and M4 is first-differencing appropriate as a stationarity-rendering transformation. In M1 no transformation is necessary, while in M3 a trend should be simultaneously estimated.

Suppose, for example, that lnS is described by M3, and that a first difference is inappropriately applied. Then:

$$\Delta \ln S_t = \beta_1^3 + \Phi_3^{-1}(L)\ \Theta_3'(L)\ \varepsilon_t$$

where $\Theta_3'(L) = (1 - L)\ \Theta_3(L)$ is noninvertible.

The incorrect assumption that a model contains trend can lead to poor forecasting results, as pointed out by Dickey, Bell and Miller (1986). To see this, recall that the minimum mean squared error linear forecast is always given by the conditional expectation:

$$\hat{y}_{T+k} = E\ (y_{T+k} \mid y_1, \ldots, y_T)\ .$$

For stationary series,

$$\hat{y}_{T+k} \dashrightarrow \mu = E\ y_t \text{ as } k \dashrightarrow \infty$$

and

$$\text{var}\ \hat{y}_{T+k} \dashrightarrow \text{var}\ y_t\ ,$$

the unconditional variance of the series.

For integrated series, on the other hand, $\hat{y}_{T+k}$ either explodes or behaves like a polynomial in k, and

$$\text{var}\ \hat{y}_{T+k} \dashrightarrow \infty\ .$$

Analogous results hold if a series is given by stationary or integrated deviations about trend.

Thus, while overdifferencing leads to noninvertibility, the parameters of the series may still be estimated in a consistent and unbiased fashion. Inappropriate trend removal, on the other hand, leads to incorrect forecasts and prediction intervals at all forecasting horizons. Thus, the reason why in the tests below the null, as opposed to the alternative, is that of a unit root is because of the relative importance of errors of differencing versus errors of not differencing. As Dickey, Bell and Miller (1986) note:

"Failure to include a differencing operator when it is needed results in bounded forecast intervals that must eventually be too narrow, giving unreasonable confidence in the forecasts, especially the long term forecasts. This can be especially true if a polynomial trend plus stationary error model is used when differencing is needed."

In order to investigate the possibility of unit roots in the autoregressive lag-operator polynomials of our exchange rate series, while nevertheless allowing for trend or nonzero mean under the alternative, a number of formal unit root tests are performed. In the appendix to this chapter we give a detailed description of all testing procedures.

Solo's (1984) test is a Lagrange multiplier (LM) test for unit roots in general ARMA models; since it is an LM test, it requires estimates only under the null of a unit root. We therefore begin by differencing the series and formulating appropriate models. Use of optimal model specification procedures, such as the Schwarz (1978) information criterion, as well as the usual diagnostics such as the sample autocorrelation function, reveal no evidence of a moving average component in any of the seven $(1 - L)\ln S_t$ series, however.[13] The simpler Dickey-Fuller test for unit roots

---

[13] The Schwarz information criterion (SIC) is a simple modification of the Akaike (1974) information criterion. Hannan (1981) has shown that it is a consistent identification procedure, in the sense that in large samples it identifies the correct model with probability one. This highly desirable property, which does not hold for the AIC, makes the SIC a powerful model specification tool. The SIC is given by:

$$SIC = \ln \hat{\sigma}_{ML} + \frac{\ln T}{T} (p + q)$$

and the model which minimizes SIC is selected.

in autoregressive series (Dickey, 1976; Fuller, 1976) is therefore employed, allowing for possible trends, nonzero means and high-order autoregressive lag operator polynomials. This test, which is a likelihood ratio test and also a Wald test, amounts to regressing $(1 - L)\ln S_t$ on an intercept, $\ln S_{t-1}$, and lags of $(1 - L)\ln S_t$ (if only a nonzero mean is allowed under the alternative) or an intercept, trend term, $\ln S_{t-1}$, and lags of $(1 - L)\ln S_t$ (if trend is allowed under the alternative).

To develop the test, consider the autoregressive representation in deviations from trend:

$$(\ln S_t - \beta_0 - \beta_1 t) + \sum_{j=1}^{p} \phi_j (\ln S_{t-j} - \beta_0 - \beta_1(t-j)) = e_t .$$

This is easily rewritten as:

$$\ln S_t = K_1 + K_2 t + \theta_1 \ln S_{t-1} + \sum_{j=2}^{p} \theta_j (\ln S_{t-j+1} - \ln S_{t-j}) + e_t$$

where:

$$K_1 = \beta_0(1 + \sum_{i=1}^{p} \phi_i) - \beta_1 \sum_{i=1}^{p} i\, \phi_i$$

$$K_2 = \beta_1(1 + \sum_{i=1}^{p} \phi_i)$$

$$\theta_1 = - \sum_{i=1}^{p} \phi_i$$

$$\theta_i = \sum_{j=i}^{p} \phi_j \qquad i = 2, \ldots, p .$$

The null hypothesis of a unit root is $\theta_1 = 1$, and the corresponding "t-statistic" is the appropriate test statistic. Subtracting $\ln S_{t-1}$ from both sides, we have:

$$\Delta \ln S_t = K_1 + K_2 t + \theta_1' \ln S_{t-1} + \sum_{j=2}^{p} \theta_j (\ln S_{t-j+1} - \ln S_{t-j}) + e_t$$

where $\theta_1' = (\theta_1 - 1)$. The null is now $\theta_1' = 0$, so that the "t-statistic" from standard regression programs may be used. The distribution of this studentized statistic has been tabulated by Dickey (1976) using Monte-Carlo methods and is reported in Fuller (1976) as $\hat{\tau}_\tau$. (It does not have the t-distribution.)

The reader may easily verify that in the simpler case in which only a nonzero mean is allowed under the alternative, we have:

$$\Delta \ln S_t = K_1' + \theta_1' \ln S_{t-1} + \sum_{j=2}^{p} \theta_j (\ln S_{t-j+1} - \ln S_{t-j}) + e_t$$

where

$$K_1' = \mu (1 + \sum_{j=1}^{p} \alpha_j)$$

and the other parameters are as defined above. The asymptotic distribution of the studentized statistic of $\hat{\theta}_1'$ differs from that of $\hat{\tau}_\tau$ and, following Dickey, we denote it by $\hat{\tau}_\mu$. Again, the percentiles are given in Fuller's book.

The results of the $\hat{\tau}_\mu$ and $\hat{\tau}_\tau$ tests are given in Tables 3.3 and 3.4, respectively. While it is desirable to allow for trend under the alternative $(\hat{\tau}_\tau)$, if, in fact, no trend is present then $\hat{\tau}_\mu$ will be a more powerful test; for this reason, the results of both tests are reported. The basic message is quite clear: each series contains a unit root, regardless of the possible presence of trend.[14] Some evidence of such trend is displayed by the CD, FF, and LIR. In addition, the small magnitude and general statistical insignificance of the θ_j , $j = 2, \ldots, p$, indicate very little serial correlation in any of the first-differenced series.

The Dickey-Fuller tests may be interpreted in several ways: First, they may be viewed as tests of a unit root(s) in the autoregressive representations of the seven exchange rates. Because we choose a cutoff lag of seven (including the unit root), the test is strictly valid only if the true processes followed by the exchange rates are AR(p), $p < 7$. Of course, if the underlying models are full ARMA processes, then the fitting of a finite AR representation can only be viewed as an approximation. Said and Dickey (1985) show, however, that even if the underlying process is a full ARMA, the AR approximation is a good one. The only issue is the appropriate degree of the AR approximation (p); they show that one should make $p = o_p(N^{-1/3})$, so that the value $p = 7$

[14] This is consistent with the results of Meese and Singleton (1982).

used here is more than adequate for N = 632.

Further tests reject conclusively the null of an additional unit root in any of the seven series. (See Tables 3.5 and 3.6.) Thus, regardless of the possible presence of linear trend, each series is appropriately made stationary by taking a first difference. To guard against deviations from nominal test size due to the pretest implications of the sequential testing procedure, a formal joint test of the null hypothesis of two unit roots is also performed.

The model (with trend allowed under the alternative) becomes:

$$\ln S_t = \beta_0 + \beta_1 t + \beta_2 \ln S_{t-1} + \beta_3 \Delta \ln S_{t-1} + \sum_{j=1}^{p-2} \delta_j \Delta^2 \ln S_{t-j} + e_t .$$

The null of two unit roots is given by:

$$(\beta_0, \beta_1, \beta_2, \beta_3)' = (0, 0, 1, 1)'$$

and the null distribution of the "F" test of this hypothesis has been tabulated by Hasza and Fuller (1979). (It does not have the F-distribution.) The results are given in Table 3.4, in the column labled "F." As expected, we reject the null for each rate, further confirming the result of one, but not two, unit roots in each series.

To summarize the results thus far, then, a wide range of diagnostic tools in both the time and frequency domains indicates that all of the log exchange rates have "integrated" time-series representations. Specifically, each rate has one unit root in its autoregressive lag operator polynomial. A first difference, then, is sufficient to render each series stationary.

Finally, for later reference it should be pointed out that Pantula (1985) shows that the asymptotic distribution of the Dickey-Fuller statistics is invariant to conditional heteroskedasticity of the autoregressive type. This is important, in the sense that while our unit root tests are tests for a special type of serial correlation, they are robust to autoregressive conditional heteroskedasticity. This is not true of standard tests for stationary serial correlation such as the Durbin-Watson test.

The differenced series appear in Figures 3.10 - 3.16. A visual inspection of these $\Delta \ln S$ series reveals no evidence of serial correlation, although there does seem to be persistence in the conditional variances, as we discuss in detail below. The sample autocorrelations are calculated for each $\Delta \ln S$ series up to lag 40, and in each case they strongly indicate white noise. The first twelve sample autocorrelations for each series are given in Table 3.7, along with their asymptotic standard errors (Bartlett, 1946).[15] For each series, all sample autocorrelations are very small, and almost all are within the Bartlett two standard error bands. The sample partial autocorrelation functions and sample inverse autocorrelation functions similarly indicate white noise. In addition, since the Bartlett "tests" are at the (approximate) 5% level, we would expect roughly 5% of the sample autocorrelations to appear significant, purely on the basis of type I errors. The actual percentage in Table 4 is 7%, which is in close agreement.

The Ljung-Box (LB) statistics, which are reported in Table 8 for lags of 6, 12, and 18, also generally indicate the absence of serial correlation, although the results are not so conclusive. Note that since no parameters have been estimated, no degrees of freedom are lost. Thus, for example, the LB statistic at lag 18 has a null distribution of χ^2_{18}. With few exceptions, for all series at all lags, the null of white noise cannot be rejected at the 1% level. At other levels the results are mixed, with some series, such as the SF, not enabling rejection at any reasonable level, and others enabling rejection. It must be remembered that due to the large sample size, it becomes very easy to reject, so that it is crucial to examine the magnitude and importance of any deviations from white noise in addition to their statistical significance. (This is in fact the reason for presenting the sample autocorrelations in Table 3.7). Indeed, from a decision-theoretic viewpoint, we should use stringent significance levels when working in large samples, in order to achieve very small probabilities of both type I and type II errors, rather than arbitrarily fixing P(type I) at, say, 5%, and letting P(type II) $\rightarrow$ 0. In fact, if conditional heteroskedasticity is present, we would expect to see large values of serial correlation test statistics, even if the series displays no serial correlation, as

---

[15] While Bartlett's standard errors depend upon normality, leptokurtic deviations from normality such as exist in the foreign exchange markets will simply make the tests more conservative.

shown in chapter 2. This view is supported by the Domowitz-Hakkio (1983) heteroskedasticity-robust LM test values shown in Table 3.9.

Spectral analyses also indicate that the first difference of each ΔlnS series is close to white noise; the estimated spectral density functions display no noticeable power concentrations in any particular frequency bands.[16] In addition, Fisher's (1929) kappa, reported in Table 3.8, does not enable rejection of the the null at any reasonable level.[17] Fisher's kappa is the ratio of the maximum to the average periodogram ordinate:

$$FK = MaxP \;/\; (\frac{SumP}{M-1})$$

where MaxP is the maximum periodogram ordinate and SumP is the sum of the M - 1 periodogram ordinates. Under the null hypothesis of independent normally distributed observations,

$$P(M^{-1}FK > g) = \sum_{j=1}^{k} (-1)^{j-1} \binom{m}{j} (1-jg)^{m-1},$$

where k is the largest integer less than g^{-1}. Tables are given in Fuller (1976), <u>inter alia</u>.

There is no indication of seasonality in any of the first differenced series, whether analyzed in the frequency or time domain. In fact, taking a seasonal difference to produce the series $(1 - L)(1 - L^{52})\ln S_t$ introduces (spurious) seasonality in all cases. The sample autocorrelation functions of $(1 - L)(1 - L^{52})\ln S_t$, for all exchange rates, display sharp and significant spikes at lag 52, whereas the earlier first differenced series did not.

Finally, in order to access the distributional properties of the ΔlnS series, a wide range of descriptive statistics is also reported in Table 3.8, including mean, variance, standard deviation, coefficient of variation, skewness, kurtosis, Kolmogorov's D statistic for the null hypothesis of normality, the Kiefer-

---

16 A simple triangular lag window was used, with weights 1/25, 2/25, ..., 7/25, 6/25, ..., 1/25.

17 The only exception is the CD, for which we do reject at the 2% level. In light of our time domain results, this is quite anomolous, and we ascribe it to a type I error.

Salmon (1983) Lagrange multiplier normality test, and a wide range of order statistics. As expected, we cannot reject the null of a zero mean, except for those series which appear to contain a linear trend in nondifferenced form (CD, FF, LIR). It is important to note also that in each case the hypothesis of normality is rejected, whether an interquartile range test, Kolmogorov's D, or the Kiefer-Salmon test is used. Evidence on the nature of deviations from normality may be gleaned from the sample skewness and kurtosis measures. While skewness of each series is always very close to zero, the kurtosis (shifted so that zero kurtosis corresponds to normality) is very large, ranging from 1.23 for the DM to 8.09 for the LIR. Normal probability plots were also generated for each series and further confirmed this finding. In addition, the Kiefer-Salmon Lagrange multiplier statistic:

$$KS = \frac{N}{6} (\hat{\mu}_3 - 3\,\hat{\mu}_1)^2 + \frac{N}{24} (\hat{\mu}_4 - 6\,\hat{\mu}_2 + 3)^2$$

$$\equiv KS_1 + KS_2$$

distributed as χ^2_2 under the null of normality, may be decomposed into two asymptotically independent χ^2_1 variates, the first being an LM test for normal skewness and the second, an LM test for normal kurtosis. The sample moments $\hat{\mu}_i$ which enter the KS statistic must be calculated from residuals standardized by $\hat{\sigma}_{ML}$, the maximum likelihood estimate of the innovation variance. The test statistics reported in Table 3.8 show the clear nonnormality of each series, most of which is due to leptokurtosis. For a fairly large fraction of the series we also reject the null of zero skewness, but as shown above the skewness is in fact negligibly small, the statistical rejection being due to large sample size.

In Table 3.10 the same test statistics are presented for the residuals from a third-order autoregression including a constant term. The results are similar, except that, as expected, the LB statistics fail to reject the null of uncorrelated disturbances for each series. We conclude that, while $\Delta \ln S$ is close to white noise for each series, any slight serial correlation present is well captured by an AR(3) model.

In conclusion, we have shown that a wide variety of techniques leads to the same result: the evolution of the conditional mean of the stochastic structures of the seven exchange rates studied are such that ΔlnS is close (in the class of linear time series models) to a random walk. We now proceed to investigate further the properties of these "random walks."

3.5) Empirical Results

The results of the LM test (TR^2 version) for ARCH in the ΔlnS series (both raw variables and AR(3) residuals) are given in Table 3.11; the existence of a strong ARCH effect in all series, with the possible exception of the FF, is clear. (The nulls of no first, second, third, fourth, and eighth order ARCH are rejected at the 1% level for each series except the FF.) Unfortunately, these tests are of little use in specifying the appropriate <u>order</u> of the ARCH processes, since they test the joint null that $\alpha_1 = \dots = \alpha_p = 0$. Thus, while they almost always reject, that does not mean that <u>all</u> the α_i's are necessarily nonzero. Likelihood ratio tests, on the other hand, enable us to test subset restrictions such as, for example, $\alpha_8 = \alpha_9 = \alpha_{10} = 0$ in an ARCH(10) model. For this reason, high order (ARCH(12)) models are estimated by maximum likelihood for each series, and likelihood-ratio tests are then used to test a wide range of exclusion restrictions. The ARCH(12) results for the seven currencies are given in Table 3.12. The Davidon-Fletcher-Powell algorithm is used to maximize the likelihoods; square roots, rather than the levels, of all ARCH parameters are estimated in order to ensure that $\alpha_0 > 0$ and $\alpha_i > 0$, for all $i = 1, \dots, p$. By the invariance property of the maximum likelihood estimator, the squared values of these estimates are the MLE's of the parameter levels.

The log likelihood was stated earlier as:

$$\ln L(\beta, \alpha; \Delta\ln S, X) = \text{const} - \sum_{t=1}^{T} \ln\sigma_t - 1/2 \sum_{t=1}^{T} \frac{\varepsilon_t^2}{\sigma_t^2} .$$

This is of course conditional on $\{\Delta\ln S_t, X_t\}_{t=-p+1}^{0}$ since, for example,

$$\sigma_1^2 = \alpha_0 + \alpha_1 \varepsilon_0^2 + \ldots + \alpha_p \varepsilon_{1-p}^2 .$$

Construction of the exact likelihood function would require knowledge of the unconditional density function of the ARCH process, a closed-form expression for which is not available. (See Pantula (1985).) However, the particular initial conditions used will be asymptotically inconsequential. We therefore follow standard practice and condition on the first p observations. The point log likelihoods are therefore summed from t = p+1 to T.

Table 3.12 shows the estimated square root parameter values (with their associated t-statistics), iterations to convergence, log likelihoods, the sums of the α_i , and the unconditional variances, $\alpha_0 / (1 - \sum_{i=1}^{p} \alpha_i)$. A wide range of ARCH (p^*), $p^* < 12$, subset models is estimated, and likelihood-ratio tests are performed to test the exclusion restrictions. All currencies have significant ARCH effects at lag 10 or higher, and, in fact, the CD, DM, and BP have significant twelfth order ARCH Effects. Although we can not reject the null of $\alpha_{11} = \alpha_{12} = 0$ for the FF, LIR, and YEN, and we can not reject the null of $\alpha_{12} = 0$ for the SF, the twelfth order specification is retained in order to maintain conformity among the models since the large number of degrees of freedom enables us to maintain the twelfth order model at little cost. Similarly, an intercept term to pick up trend and three lags of $\Delta \ln S$ to pick up any serial correlation present in any of the series are included. Although our earlier results show little, if any, serial correlation, it is important that it be modeled, if present, in order to avoid confusion with ARCH effects. Again, there is little cost in terms of lost degrees of freedom. Thus, the models which were estimated are all third order AR representations (with allowance for a nonzero mean) with twelfth-order ARCH disturbances:

$$(1 - \rho_1 L - \rho_2 L^2 - \rho_3 L^3) (\Delta \ln S_t - \mu) = \varepsilon_t$$

$$\varepsilon_t | \varepsilon_{t-1}, \ldots, \varepsilon_{t-12} \sim N (0, \sigma_t^2)$$

$$\sigma_t^2 = \alpha_0 + \sum_{i=1}^{12} \alpha_i \varepsilon_{t-i}^2 .$$

As expected, the intercept and AR parameters are often insignificant and always very small, while many of the ARCH parameters are highly significant and of substantial magnitude. The intercept term is insignificant for all exchange rates; the CD, FF and LIR, which had significant means according to the t-tests presented in Table 3, now do not. This difference is due to the fact that we have now modeled the conditional heteroskedasticity, as well as the slight serial correlation, that appears in each of those series. All but one of the twenty-one autoregressive lag coefficients for the seven currencies are positive, all are very small, and most are insignificant, as expected. The currencies with significant autoregressive terms are the CD, LIR and YEN, each of which has two significant lags.

All of the $\sqrt{\alpha_0}$ coefficients are highly significant for each series, and they are substantially smaller then the sample standard deviations shown in Table 4, or the standard errors of the innovations from classical AR(3) models. This is because the lagged squared innovations make a large contribution to the conditional variance, as indicated by the large number of significant $\sqrt{\alpha_i}$ coefficients, and the resulting ARCH effects also boost the unconditional variance.

Convergence is obtained for each exchange rate in no more than thirty iterations, where the initial conditions for maximum likelihood iteration are given by the least squares estimates. Furthermore, the log likelihood was noticeably single-peaked, leading to the same parameter estimates regardless of initial conditions. It is of interest to note the substantial number of significant ARCH coefficients for the FF (and their sum of .7), in spite of the fact that the earlier LM test indicated little ARCH. Also, the LIR ARCH parameters sum to 1.258, indicating nonexistence of unconditional second moment.[18]

Engle (1982b) and Engle, Lilien, and Robins (1987) argue on a priori grounds that the α_i, $i = 1, \ldots, p$ should be monotonically decreasing. This follows from the basic intuition of the ARCH model, which is that high volatility "today" tends to be followed

---

[18] It should be noted that most of the implied unconditional moments are somewhat larger than their counterparts from Table 3. This may be due to the overpara meterized nature of the models, which can only increase the implied unconditional variance, since all ARCH parameters are constrained to be positive.

by similar volatility "tomorrow," and vice versa. In this spirit, it is unreasonable to let a squared innovation from the distant past have a greater effect on current conditional variance than a squared innovation from the recent past. This intuition may be enforced by restricting the α_i, $i = 1...p$ to be monotonically decreasing. Both "Fisher lags" (linearly declining weights) and geometric lags are explored. Note that both of these are two parameter models, as follows:

Linear

$$\sigma_t^2 | \varepsilon_{t-1}, \ldots, \varepsilon_{t-p} = \alpha_0 + \theta \; [p \; \varepsilon_{t-1}^2 + (p-1) \; \varepsilon_{t-2}^2 + \ldots + \varepsilon_{t-p}^2]$$

Geometric

$$\sigma_t^2 | \; \varepsilon_{t-1} \ldots \varepsilon_{t-p} = \alpha_0 + \theta \varepsilon_{t-1}^2 + \ldots + \theta^p \varepsilon_{t-p}^2 \; .$$

The estimates of the linearly constrained ARCH models are given in Table 3.13. Use of the maximized log likelihoods of the linearly constrained and unconstrained models to construct formal likelihood-ratio tests statistics (distributed χ_{11}^2 under the null that the linearly restricted model holds) shows that the data generally do not strongly reject the restriction. This stands in marked contrast to the geometrically constrained model, which is decisively rejected for all exchange rates. The geometric weights simply decrease too quickly, while the linear weights allow a slower decline. Inspection of Table 8 reveals that the estimates and significance of μ, ρ_1, ρ_2, and ρ_3 are little changed, and, as before, the estimates of $\sqrt{\alpha_0}$ are highly significant. In addition, all $\sqrt{\theta}$ estimates are highly significant and range from .08 to .12. Furthermore, for each exchange rate, the sum of the implied lag weights, given by 78 $\hat{\theta}$, is slightly smaller than the corresponding figure for the unconstrained model, leading to a smaller unconditional innovation variance. This occurs because the linearly decreasing lag weights remove the influence of occasional large unconstrained α_i estimates at high lags.

The estimated conditional variances are easily obtained. We begin with the estimated disturbances:

$$\hat{\varepsilon}_{jt} = \Delta\ln S_{jt} - \hat{con}_j - \hat{\rho}_{1j}\,\Delta\ln S_{j,t-1} - \hat{\rho}_{2j}\,\Delta\ln S_{j,t-2} - \hat{\rho}_{3j}\Delta\ln S_{j,t-3}$$

j = CD, FF, DM, LIR, YEN,SF, BP.

The estimated conditional variance is then given by:

$$\hat{\sigma}^2_{jt} = \hat{\alpha}_{0j} + \sum_{i=1}^{12} \hat{\alpha}_{ij}\,\hat{\varepsilon}^2_{j,t-i}.$$

j = CD, FF, DM, LIR, YEN,SF, BP.

The time series of estimated conditional variances from the constrained ARCH(12) model are graphed below in Figures 3.17 - 3.23.

While there are substantial "own country" effects in the movements of the conditional variance of each rate, similarities in the qualitative conditional variance movements are apparent. There is a tendency toward high conditional variance in the very early part of the float, due largely to the uncertainty created by the 70% increase in the posted price of Arabian crude oil of October 16, 1973, and the additional 100% increase of December 24. As we progress to the middle of the 1970's we see generally smaller conditional variances as the gloomy economic news translated into relatively smooth dollar depreciation, culminating in the historic lows achieved against the DM, YEN and other major currencies on December 29, 1977. The year 1978, particularly the latter part, brings a return of higher volatility, as large intervention efforts by the Federal Reserve and the Treasury begin to turn the dollar around. The further OPEC three-stage 14.5% crude oil price boost increases economic uncertainty, and the year ends with widespread ression forcasts in spite of a still (relatively) vigorous economy. Another period of very high conditional variances arises in mid-1981, as interest rates in the 20% range bring the dollar to new highs against the major European currencies. The CD also reaches a post-1931 low on July 31, closing at 80.9 U.S. cents. As inflation subsides, so too does exchange rate volatility, but it does begin to grow again toward the end of the sample.

The ARCH-based prediction intervals clearly capture and exploit these movements in conditional variance. As an example, the $\Delta \ln S_{DM}$ series is plotted in figure 3.24, along with its ARCH-based $2\hat{\sigma}_t$ and its classical $2\hat{\sigma}$ 1-step ahead prediction intervals. The classical $2\hat{\sigma}$ bands are basically time-invariant and horizontal at ± 3%. Some high-frequency movement in the classical bands occurs, of course, due to the slight serial correlation which produces slightly changing 1-step ahead point forecasts. Movements in the ARCH-based prediction intervals are more systematic, being much tighter in tranquil times and wider in more volatile periods.

3.6) Conclusions

We show that the percentage changes of nominal dollar spot exchange rates under the recent floating rate regime have approximate random-walk conditional mean behavior but contain substantial nonlinearities which manifest themselves in the form of ARCH effects in the conditional variance. This leads to economically and statistically meaningful measures of exchange rate volatility, explains the leptokurtosis which has previously been found in the distribution of exchange rate changes, and enables the construction of superior prediction intervals.

Table 3.1
Weekly Nominal Dollar Spot Rates
Sample Autocorrelations For lnS

Lag	CD	FF	DM	LIR	YEN	SF	BP
1	.99	1.00	.99	.99	.99	1.00	.99
2	.99	.99	.99	.99	.99	.99	.99
3	.98	.99	.98	.98	.98	.98	.98
4	.98	.98	.97	.98	.97	.98	.98
5	.97	.97	.97	.97	.97	.97	.97
6	.97	.97	.96	.97	.96	.97	.96
7	.96	.96	.95	.96	.95	.96	.96
8	.96	.96	.95	.96	.94	.95	.95
9	.95	.95	.94	.95	.93	.95	.94
10	.95	.94	.93	.95	.93	.94	.93
11	.94	.94	.92	.94	.92	.93	.92
12	.94	.94	.92	.93	.91	.92	.92

Table 3.2
Weekly Nominal Dollar Spot Rates
Sample Partial Autocorrelations For lnS

Lag	CD	FF	DM	LIR	YEN	SF	BP
1	.99	1.00	.99	.99	.99	1.00	.99
2	-.02	.04	-.03	.01	-.08	-.07	.05
3	-.02	-.08	-.10	-.05	-.10	-.01	-.02
4	.01	.00	-.02	.03	-.06	-.03	.00
5	.01	-.02	-.03	-.02	-.03	-.06	-.06
6	-.00	-.03	-.05	-.03	.00	-.04	-.06
7	-.00	.04	.06	.00	.02	-.04	.01
8	.01	.01	-.00	-.03	-.00	.02	-.02
9	-.01	-.03	-.06	-.02	.03	-.02	-.06
10	.01	-.01	-.02	-.00	-.01	-.01	.03
11	-.02	-.02	-.03	-.01	.06	-.04	.01
12	.01	-.01	-.03	-.01	.01	.01	-.02

Table 3.3
Weekly Nominal Dollar Spot Rates
Test For Unit Root in lnS, Nonzero Mean Allowed Under the Alternative

ΔlnS	const	lnS(-1)	ΔlnS(-1)	ΔlnS(-2)	ΔlnS(-3)	ΔlnS(-4)	ΔlnS(-5)	ΔlnS(-6)
CD	.00047	-.00008	.11020	.07363	-.93947	-.08294	-.00044	-.03537
	(1.40)	(-.04)*	(2.73)***	(1.82)*	(-.34)	(-2.05)**	(-.01)	(-.88)
FF	.00001	.00061	.04886	.10077	.05169	.00120	-.073743	-.06666
	(.00)	(.30)**	(1.22)	(2.52)***	(1.28)*	(.03)	(-1.84)*	(-1.67)*
DM	.0286	-.00312	.07045	.06419	.03954	.01077	-.00179	-.07191
	(.94)	(-.89)	(1.77)*	(1.60)*	(.98)	(.27)	(-.04)	(-1.81)*
LIR	.00095	.00011	.01961	.07926	.09217	.01109	-.07886	-.02507
	(.10)	(.08)*	(.49)	(1.97)**	(2.25)**	(.27)	(-1.93)*	(-.61)
YEN	.03504	-.00637	.06043	.10695	.05718	.05221	-.00315	-.02854
	(1.60)	(-1.61)	(1.50)	(2.66)***	(1.41)	(1.28)	(-.08)	(-.70)
SF	.00427	-.00589	.05805	.02279	.04091	.04124	.02275	-.02140
	(1.60)	(-1.79)	(1.45)	(.56)	(1.00)	(1.01)	(.56)	(-.53)
BP	.00034	-.00191	.03027	.02500	.04710	.10210	-.00627	-.05500
	(.19)	(-.71)	(.74)	(.61)	(1.16)	(2.52)***	(-.15)	(-1.33)

* Significant at the 10% level
** Significant at the 5% level
*** Significant at the 2% level

TABLE 3.4
Weekly Nominal Dollar Spot Rates
Test For Unit Root in lnS, Trend Allowed Under the Alternative

ΔlnS	Const	t	lnS(-1)	ΔlnS(-1)	ΔlnS(-2)	ΔlnS(-3)	ΔlnS(-4)	ΔlnS(-5)	ΔlnS(-6)	F
CD	-.00075	.00001	-.02084	.11783	.08271	-.00459	-.07391	.00822	-.02566	31.40***
	(-1.37)	(2.84)***	(-2.74)	(2.93)***	(2.05)**	(-.11)	(-1.83)*	(.20)	(-.64)	
FF	.00485	.00001	-.00383	.04921	.10116	.05292	.00274	-.07274	-.06526	30.90***
	(1.08)	(1.71)*	(-1.16)	(1.23)	(2.53)***	(1.32)	(.07)	(-1.81)*	(-1.64)*	
DM	.00225	.00000	-.00399	.06911	.06280	.03898	.00972	-.00383	-.07355	28.34***
	(.73)	(1.39)	(-1.12)	(1.73)*	(1.56)	(.97)	(.24)	(-.10)	(-1.85)*	
LIR	.04200	.00001	-.00648	.02216	.08162	.09472	.01442	-.07538	-.02162	26.71***
	(1.52)	(1.58)	(-1.47)	(.55)	(2.03)**	(2.32)**	(.35)	(-1.84)*	(-.53)	
YEN	.04974	-.00000	-.00885	.06129	.10792	.05832	.05379	-.00111	-.02641	22.84***
	(1.85)*	(-.95)	(-1.86)	(1.52)	(2.68)***	(1.44)	(1.32)	(-.03)	(-.65)	
SF	.00215	.00000	-.00458	.05642	.02065	.03899	.03881	.01988	-.02416	24.49***
	(.59)	(.86)	(-1.26)	(1.40)	(.51)	(.96)	(.95)	(.48)	(-.59)	
BP	.00404	-.00001	-.00522	.03156	.02635	.04873	.10393	-.00441	-.05311	23.70***
	(1.11)	(-1.17)	(-1.33)	(.77)	(.65)	(1.20)	(2.56)***	(-.11)	(-1.28)	

* significant at 10% level
** significant at 5% level
*** significant at 2% level

Table 3.5
Weekly Nominal Dollar Spot Rates
Test For Unit root in $\Delta \ln S$

$\Delta^2 \ln S$	$\Delta \ln S(-1)$	$\Delta^2 \ln S(-2)$	$\Delta^2 \ln S(-3)$	$\Delta^2 \ln S(-3)$	$\Delta^2 \ln S(-4)$	$\Delta^2 \ln S(-5)$	$\Delta^2 \ln S(-6)$
CD	-.95671 (-10.18)***	.07267 (.84)	.15302 (1.94)*	.14020 (1.98)**	.06178 (.98)	.07139 (1.33)	.04929 (1.22)
FF	-.88617 (-9.61)***	-.05256 (-.62)	.05338 (.68)	.11287 (1.57)	.12016 (1.85)*	.04211 (.75)	-.00583 (-.14)
DM	-.85727 (-9.18)***	-.07012 (-.81)	.00016 (.00)	.04216 (.57)	.05316 (.81)	.04725 (.85)	-.03847 (-.94)
LIR	-.69468 (-7.91)***	-.26714 (-3.25)***	-.16358 (-2.15)**	-.06268 (-.88)	.05401 (-.84)	-.13957 (-2.52)***	-.15352 (-3.79)***
YEN	-.77272 (-8.74)***	-.16876 (-2.03)**	-.06393 (-.82)	-.00975 (-.13)	.03917 (.60)	.03204 (.58)	-.00059 (-.01)
SF	-.85506 (-8.97)***	-.08768 (-.98)	-.06225 (-.74)	-.02072 (-.27)	.02083 (.31)	.04295 (.76)	.01654 (.40)
BP	-.78678 (-8.28)***	-.17572 (-1.96)**	-.14812 (-1.76)*	-.11010 (-1.40)	-.00969 (-.14)	-.01411 (-.24)	-.07008 (-1.69)*

* Significant ant the 10% level
** Significant at the 5% level
*** Significant at the 2% level

Table 3.6
Weekly Nominal Dollar Spot Rates
Test For Unit Root in $\Delta \ln S$,
Nonzero Mean Allowed Under the Alternative

$\Delta^2 \ln S$	c	$\Delta \ln S(-1)$	$\Delta^2 \ln S(-1)$	$\Delta^2 \ln S(-2)$	$\Delta^2 \ln S(-3)$	$\Delta^2 \ln S(-4)$	$\Delta^2 \ln S(-5)$	$\Delta^2 \ln S(-6)$
CD	.00049 (2.28)**	-1.00360 (10.46)***	.11176 (1.27)	.18546 (2.32)**	.16668 (2.34)***	.08275 (1.31)	.08621 (1.60)	.05727 (1.42)*
FF	.00106 (1.92)*	-.92034 (-9.82)***	-.02409 (-.28)	.07663 (.97)	.13233 (1.82)*	.13579 (2.07)**	.05331 (.95)	-.00001 (-.00012)
DM	.00021 (.38)	-.85890 (-9.18)***	-.06870 (-.79)	.00137 (.02)	.04322 (.59)	.05402 (.82)	.04783 (.86)	-.03817 (-.93)
LIR	.00156 (2.98)***	-.78415 (-8.50)***	-.19316 (-2.27)**	-.10441 (-1.34)	-.01465 (-.20)	-.01583 (-.24)	-.11245 (-2.02)**	-.13979 (-3.45)***
YEN	-.00013 (-.25)	-.77329 (-8.74)***	-.16831 (-2.02)**	-.06358 (-.81)	-.00950 (-.13)	.03935 (.60)	.03218 (.58)	-.00052 (-.01)
SF	-.00034 (-.53)	-.85773 (-8.98)***	-.08558 (-.95)	-.06056 (-.72)	-.01949 (-.25)	.02171 (.32)	.04356 (.77)	.01687 (.41)
BP	-.00081 (-1.47)	-.81026 (-8.41)***	-.15550 (-1.72)*	-.13084 (-1.54)	-.09561 (1.21)	.00155 (.02)	-.00642 (-.11)	-.06613 (-1.59)*

* Significant at the 10% level
** Significant at the 5% level
*** Significant at the 2% level

TABLE 3.7
Weekly Nominal Dollar Spot Rates
Sample Autocorrelations And Bartlett's Standard Errors, ΔlnS

LAG	CD	FF	DM	LIR	YEN	SF	BP
1	.119*	.048	.068	.019	.075	.054	.035
	(.040)	(.040)	(.040)	(.040)	(.040)	(.040)	(.040)
2	.081*	.108*	.065	.079	.116*	.033	.022
	(.040)	(.040)	(.040)	(.040)	(.040)	(.040)	(.040)
3	-.006	.067	.047	.087*	.070	.049	.049
	(.041)	(.040)	(.040)	(.040)	(.040)	(.040)	(.040)
4	-.082	-.005	.003	.012	.064	.034	.101
	(.041)	(.041)	(.041)	(.041)	(.041)	(.041)	(.041)
5	-.025	-.044	.010	-.058	.012	.040	.001
	(.041)	(.041)	(.041)	(.041)	(.041)	(.041)	(.041)
6	-.050	-.066	-.069	-.018	-.016	-.016	-.046
	(.041)	(.041)	(.041)	(.041)	(.041)	(.041)	(.041)
7	-.065	-.019	.018	.117*	.005	-.014	.069
	(.041)	(.041)	(.041)	(.041)	(.041)	(.041)	(.041)
8	.002	.021	.021	-.034	.032	.029	.077
	(.041)	(.041)	(.041)	(.041)	(.041)	(.041)	(.041)
9	-.045	.012	.029	-.020	-.005	.030	-.053
	(.041)	(.041)	(.041)	(.041)	(.041)	(.041)	(.041)
10	-.008	.076	.037	.054	-.071	.053	.005
	(.041)	(.041)	(.041)	(.041)	(.041)	(.041)	(.041)
11	.023	.028	.024	.035	-.026	-.009	.006
	(.041)	(.041)	(.041)	(.041)	(.041)	(.041)	(.041)
12	.019	.050	.051	.002	.016	.042	.067
	(.041)	(.041)	(.041)	(.041)	(.041)	(.041)	(.041)

* Exceeds two standard errors.

TABLE 3.8
Weekly Nominal Dollar Spot Rates
Test Statistics, ΔlnS

STATISTIC	CD	FF	DM	LIR	YEN	SF	BP
LB(6)	19.47***	15.80**	10.11	11.52*	18.00***	5.99	10.52
LB(12)	24.13**	22.28**	13.86	23.98**	22.53**	10.23	22.08**
LB(18)	26.44*	24.83	21.20	34.30***	35.13***	15.95	31.10**
M-1	315	315	315	315	315	315	315
MaxP	.001	.002	.002	.002	.002	.002	.002
SumP	.017	.122	.120	.100	.103	.169	.117
FK	12.175***	4.888	5.172	4.797	6.589	4.358	5.643
Mean	.00049	.00126	.00034	.00189	-.00017	-.00024	-.00104
t (μ=0)	2.35**	2.28**	.61	3.77***	-.33	-.37	-1.92*
Variance	.00003	.00019	.00019	.00016	.00016	.00027	.00018
Std. Dev.	.00526	.01390	.01381	.01260	.01276	.01640	.01360
CV	1068.27	1100.66	4078.43	666.63	-7532.13	-6848.97	-1310.93
Skewness	.56098	.26069	-.08594	.44196	-.21592	-.1072	.34407
Kurtosis	4.70565	2.53659	1.23452	8.08811	3.26364	1.495	3.2979
D	.070***	.07121***	.056***	.093***	.10769***	.0554***	.072***
KS	633.61***	178.99***	38.97***	1667.12***	280.55***	58.74***	268.34***
KS1	31.90***	6.86***	.77	18.54***	4.88**	1.20	12.24***
KS2	601.71***	172.13***	38.20***	1648.58***	275.67***	57.54***	256.1***
Maximum	.03754	.07478	.05776	.09679	.06980	.06616	.07246
Q3	.00309	.00788	.00826	.00725	.00641	.00892	.00543
Median	.00067	.00070	.00050	.00061	.00030	.00039	-.00058
Q1	-.00240	-.00545	-.00732	-.00373	-.00520	-.00872	-.00839
Minimum	-.01762	-.04583	-.04839	-.07490	-.05671	-.05421	-.05322
Mode	0	0	0	0	0	0	0
SR	10.49***	8.68***	7.69***	13.63***	9.91***	7.34***	9.24***

NOTES: LB(N) = Ljung-Box statistic at lag N
M-1 = number of independent periodogram ordinates
MaxP = maximum periodogram ordinate, MinP = minimum periodogram ordinate
SumP = sum of periodogram ordinates
FK = Fisher's kappa
CV = coefficient of variation
D = Kolmogorov's D for the null hypothesis of normality
KS = Kiefer-Salmon normality test, decomposed into KS1 (skewness test) and KS2 (kurtosis test)
SR = Studentized Range
Significance levels: * = 10%, ** = 5%, *** = 1%

Table 3.9
Weekly Nominal Dollar Spot Rates
Domowitz-Hakkio Heteroskedasticity-Robust Serial Correlation Tests, $\Delta \ln S$

Order	CD	FF	DM	LIR	YEN	SF	BP
One	4.44*	1.11	2.11	.09	2.46	1.39	.40
Three	7.00*	8.56**	3.84	5.99	8.38**	2.38	1.68
Eight	12.60	15.51**	8.79	10.76	12.08	4.85	7.12
Twelve	13.20	19.44*	11.31	15.01	14.28	7.08	10.11

* Significant at 10% level
** Significant at 5% level
*** Significant at 1% Level

GERMANY

Weekly Nominal Dollar Spot Rates
Test Statistics, $\Delta \ln S$ **AR(3) Residuals**

Statistic	CD	FF	DM	LIR	YEN	SF	BP
LB6	5.35*	6.84**	4.61*	5.15*	1.86	1.55	7.73**
LB12	9.62	11.82	7.72	18.79**	7.06	5.40	19.22**
LB18	11.61	14.79	16.11	28.99**	21.11*	12.30	28.30**
M-1	313	313	313	313	313	313	313
MaxP	.001	.002	.003	.002	.002	.003	.002
SumP	.017	.116	.115	.097	.100	.165	.115
FK	11.50***	4.98	7.20	5.16	6.68	5.02	4.97
Variance	.00003	.00018	.00018	.00016	.00016	.00026	.00018
Std. Dev.	.00523	.01359	.01356	.01245	.01265	.01624	.01359
Skewness	.38285	.18860	-.09304	.35371	-.17610	-.04691	.30513
Kurtosis	4.03491	2.49136	1.38697	8.26591	3.67942	1.63186	3.19811
KS	432.63***	162.32***	49.76***	1768.62***	350.06***	68.00***	271.53***
KS1	15.27***	3.71*	.90	13.03***	3.23*	.23	9.70***
KS2	417.36***	158.61***	48.86***	1755.59***	346.83***	67.77***	261.83***
D	.06806***	.06986***	.05830***	.09548***	.09519***	.05496***	.07293***
SR	10.143***	8.618	8.035***	13.659***	10.274***	7.405***	9.205***
Max	.03516	.07164	.06168	.09245	.06969	.06831	.07185
Q3	.00275	.00649	.00748	.00536	.00625	.00866	.00663
Med	.00003	-.00031	.00002	-.00126	.00057	.00059	.00029
Q1	-.00275	.00673	-.06995	-.00542	-.00545	-.00867	-.00693
Min	-.01789	-.04548	-.04727	-.07760	-.06028	-.05194	-.05325
Mode	-.00375	-.00892	-.00989	-.01922	.00158	-.00077	-.00866

NOTES: LB(N) = Ljung-Box statistic at lag N (distributed $\chi^2(N-4)$ under the null)
M-1 = number of independent periodogram ordinates
MaxP = maximum periodogram ordinate, MinP = minimum periodogram ordinate
SumP = sum of periodogram ordinates
FK = Fisher's kappa
CV = coefficient of variation
D = Kolmogorov's D for the null hypothesis of normality
KS = Kiefer-Salmon normality test, decomposed into KS1 (skewness test) and KS2 (kurtosis test)
Significance levels: * = 10%, ** = 5%, *** = 1%

Table 3.11
Weekly Nominal Dollar Spot Rates
ARCH Test Statistics, $\Delta \ln S$

	CD	FF	DM	LIR	YEN	SF	BP
Observed Time Series							
ARCH(1)	21.67***	3.67*	9.81***	20.17***	4.41***	8.60***	22.96***
ARCH(2)	21.97***	2.82	12.84***	20.05***	9.85***	15.91***	22.94***
ARCH(3)	21.94***	5.53	22.66***	24.36***	10.19**	32.14***	36.69***
ARCH(4)	19.98***	3.29	21.49***	24.85***	14.32***	41.11***	27.43***
ARCH(8)	23.55***	12.34	38.12***	110.82***	23.06***	73.40***	73.36***
ARCH(12)	25.57***	14.35	46.16***	120.94***	26.51***	83.80***	89.06***
AR(3) Residuals							
ARCH(1)	35.13***	2.28*	5.98***	23.59***	3.12*	9.41***	26.30***
ARCH(2)	35.39***	2.49	10.62***	23.56***	6.94**	16.48***	26.42***
ARCH(3)	35.33***	4.19	15.93***	26.45***	7.25*	31.92***	37.17***
ARCH(4)	36.00***	5.66	19.00***	26.77***	9.54**	57.95***	64.39***
ARCH(8)	36.56***	13.40	35.98***	118.55***	16.53**	76.37***	74.22***
ARCH(12)	38.40***	15.34	44.48***	129.50***	21.47**	88.25***	88.50***

* Significant at 10% level
** Significant at 5% level
*** Significant at 1% level

Table 3.12
Weekly Nominal Dollar Spot Rates
Unconstrained ARCH Models

Param.	CD	FF	DM	LIR	YEN	SF	BP
μ	.00029	.00081	-.00043	.00050	-.00060	-.00033	-.00083
	(1.60)	(1.54)	(-.93)	(1.65)*	(-1.37)	(-.64)	(-1.81)*
ρ_1	.10735	.04724	.09340	.08357	.08896	.07512	.06648
	(2.45)**	(1.01)	(2.29)**	(1.96)**	(1.98)**	(1.75)*	(1.48)
ρ_2	.08509	.07539	.06775	06192	.04068	.04329	.04717
	(2.14)**	(1.79)*	(1.51)	(1.44)	(.97)	(1.07)	(1.11)
ρ_3	.00325	.05607	-.02329	.09378	.08894	.03917	.04562
	(.08)	(1.30)	(-.53)	(2.23)**	(2.14)**	(.97)	(1.14)
$\sqrt{\alpha_0}$	.00292	.00798	.00655	.00341	.00743	.00632	.00720
	(8.75)***	(9.93)***	(7.48)***	(6.41)***	(13.96)***	(6.01)***	(11.04)***
$\sqrt{\alpha_1}$	.55635	.43177	.29254	.65310	.33195	.38972	.34486
	(9.04)***	(5.46)***	(3.34)***	(8.20)***	(4.29)***	(5.28)***	(5.87)***
$\sqrt{\alpha_2}$	.14090	.15868	.45147	.55900	.26705	.28082	.30620
	(1.37)	(.89)	(5.59)***	(8.17)***	(2.85)***	(2.99)***	(3.76)***
$\sqrt{\alpha_3}$	-.00002	.31895	.35379	.35975	.15020	.30538	.00000
	(-.00)	(3.62)***	(4.37)***	(4.92)***	(1.86)**	(3.03)***	(.00)
$\sqrt{\alpha_4}$	.32834	-.00000	-.00000	.15369	.28191	.33289	.34893
	(4.86)***	(-.00)	(-.00)	(1.80)*	(3.24)***	(4.19)***	(4.94)***
$\sqrt{\alpha_5}$	.12422	.31259	.00000	.24248	.24484	.30472	.00000
	(1.10)	(3.50)***	(.00)	(2.66)***	(2.61)***	(3.10)***	(.00)
$\sqrt{\alpha_6}$	.00001	.31239	.03006	.00000	.00000	.00003	.22088
	(.00)	(2.16)**	(.06)	(.00)	(.00)	(.00)	(1.78)*
$\sqrt{\alpha_7}$	.31080	.32720	.29056	.47664	-.00000	.25018	.16109
	(4.21)***	(3.91)***	(3.83)***	(8.39)***	(-.00)	(2.44)**	(1.39)
$\sqrt{\alpha_8}$	.11691	.23026	.19286	-.00000	.36969	-.00001	.00000
	(.98)	(2.34)**	(2.35)**	(-.00)	(4.53)***	(-.00)	(.00)
$\sqrt{\alpha_9}$	.19397	.21474	.18796	-.00003	.39725	.43288	.46185
	(1.75)*	(1.80)*	(1.51)	(-.00)	(5.44)***	(6.41)***	(4.91)***
$\sqrt{\alpha_{10}}$	.00002	.14527	.29665	.28320	.26026	-.00001	.05723
	(.00)	(2.14)**	(3.57)***	(4.06)***	(2.89)***	(-.00)	(.29)
$\sqrt{\alpha_{11}}$	.00000	-.00000	.19583	-.00001	.09300	.37875	.19907
	(.00)	(-.00)	(1.55)	(-.00)	(.51)	(4.15)***	(2.33)**
$\sqrt{\alpha_{12}}$	.39944	-.00000	.36131	.00000	-.00002	.18773	.33912
	(5.99)***	(-.00)	(4.85)***	(.00)	(-.00002)	(.151)	(4.59)***
iter	26	25	27	27	30	26	26
LnL	2968.654	2372.429	2385.238	2513.282	2423.545	2289.342	2396.492
$\Sigma\alpha i$	.760	.736	.829	1.258	.714	.956	.78
σ^2	.000036	.000241	.000251	N/A	.000193	.000914	.000236

Significance levels: * 10%, **5%, ***1%

Table 3.13
Weekly Nominal Dollar Spot Rates
Constrained ARCH Models

	CD	FF	DM	LIR	YEN	SF	BP
μ	.00029	.00077	-.00016	.00065	-.00021	-.00023	-.00088
	(1.48)	(1.61)	(-.33)	(2.10)*	(-.46)	(-.42)	(-1.81)*
ρ_1	.12436	.06323	.09167	.06318	.05542	.06323	.05452
	(2.81)***	(1.48)	(2.20)**	(1.49)	(1.22)	(1.49)	(1.24)
ρ_2	.07845	.09044	.07200	.06785	.07959	.03115	.03981
	(1.81)*	(2.11)**	(1.71)*	(1.52)	(1.77)*	(.72)	(.90)
ρ_3	-.02651	.05090	-.00239	.06138	.08140	.02060	.04679
	(-.60)	(1.21)	(-.06)	(1.38)	(1.78)*	(.48)	(1.06)
$\sqrt{\alpha_0}$	.00364	.00797	.00731	.00367	.00803	.00761	.00800
	(11.90)***	(10.12)***	(8.69)***	(6.27)***	(13.72)***	(7.20)***	(13.65)***
$\sqrt{\theta}$	.08372	.09664	.09912	.12287	.09184	.10505	.09430
	(10.00)***	(12.97)***	(13.72)***	(20.37)***	(13.89)***	(14.96)***	(15.74)***
iter	12	12	11	12	11	11	11
-lnL	2945.092	2368.180	2374.931	2489.467	2409.401	2278.446	2384.038
$\Sigma\alpha_i$	.547	.728	.766	1.178	.658	.861	.694
$\alpha_0/1-\Sigma\alpha_i$	.000029	.000234	.000228	NA	.000189	.000417	.000209

Significance levels: * 10%, **5%, ***1%

Figure 3.1

ONE HUNDRED N(0,1) OBSERVATIONS

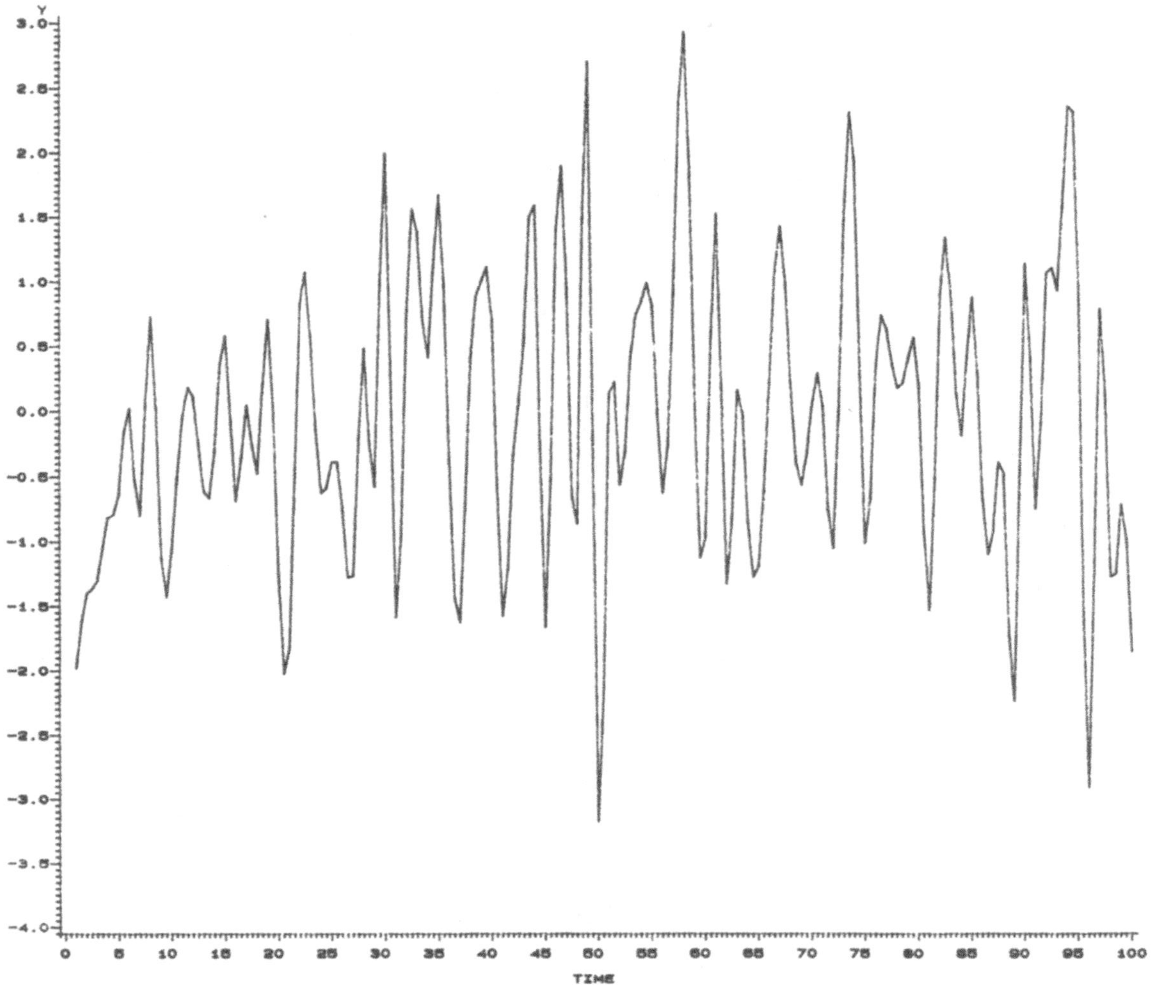

Figure 3.2

MOVING SAMPLE VARIANCE

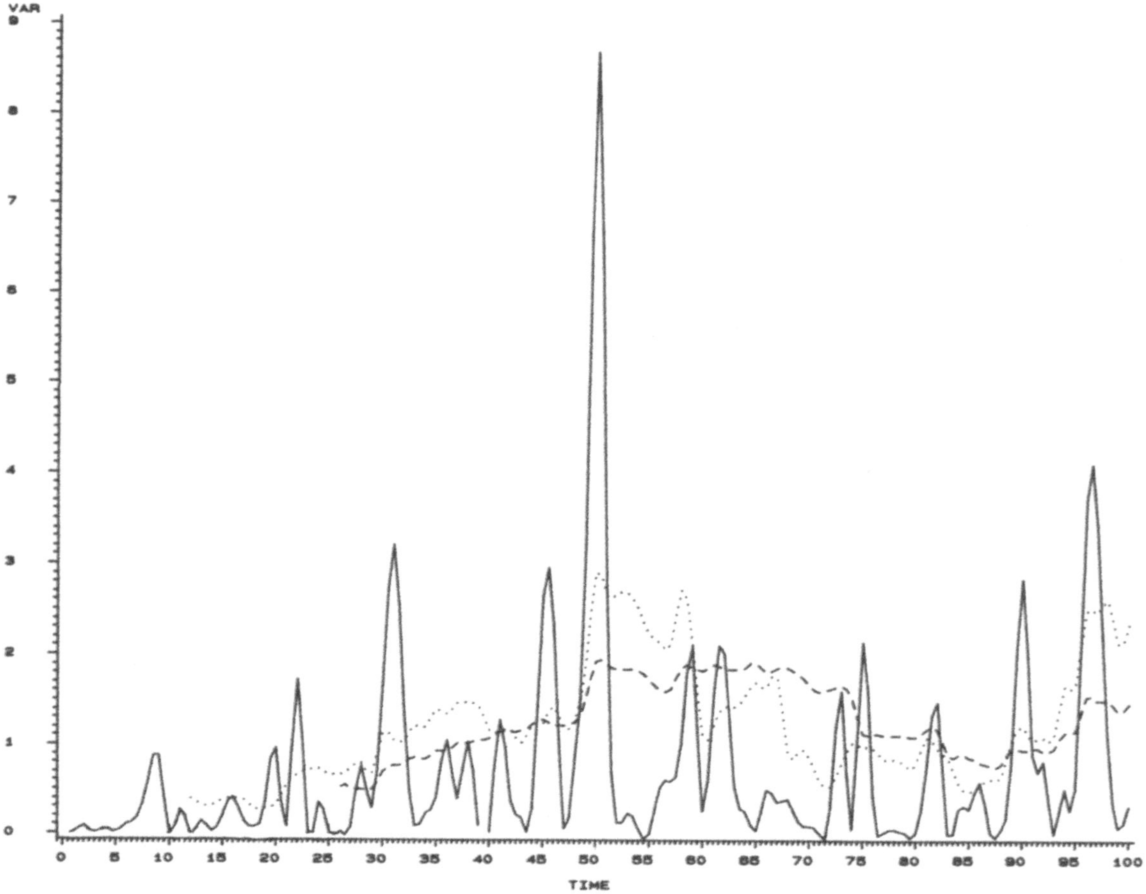

SOLID=2-PERIOD, DOT=10-PERIOD, DASH=25 PERIOD

Figure 3.3

LOG DM/DOLLAR RATE

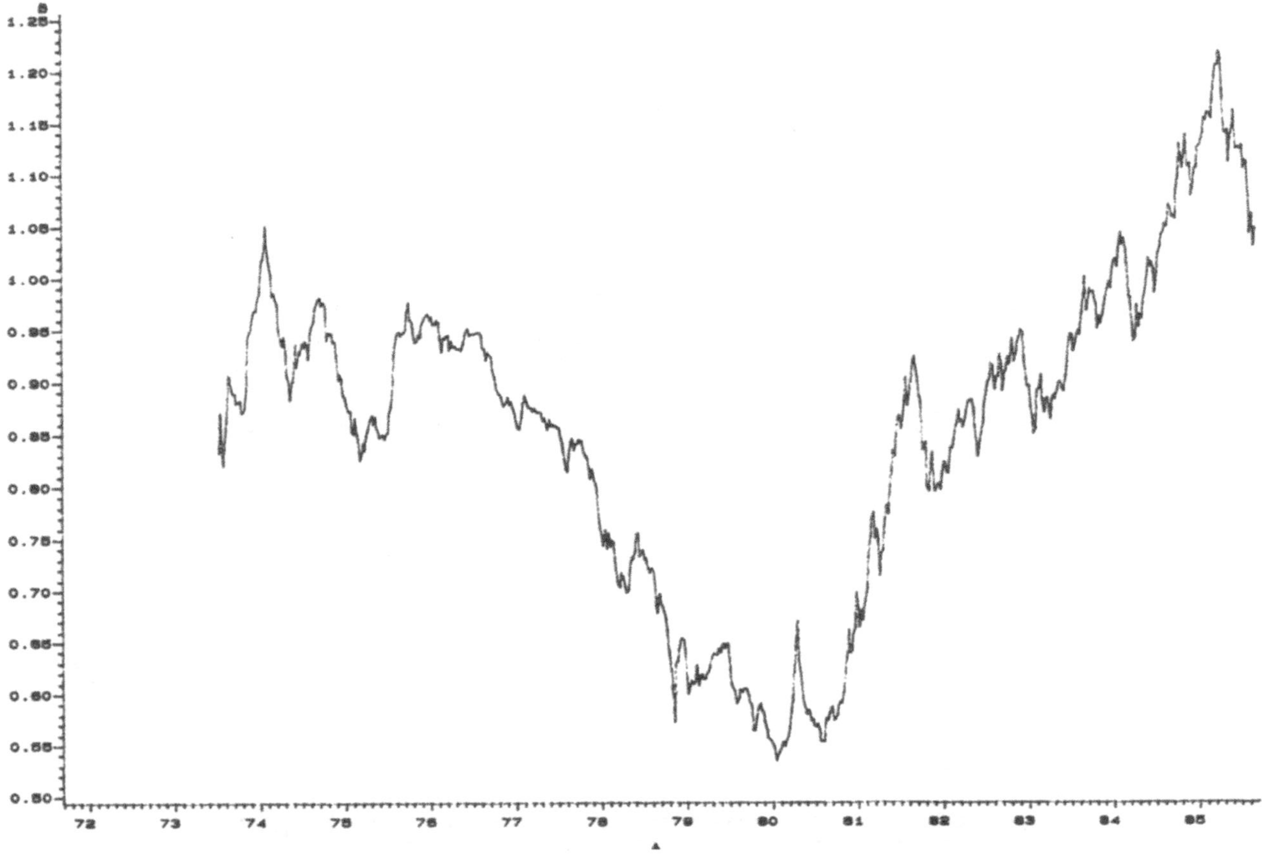

Figure 3.4

LOG DM/DOLLAR RATE, FIRST DIFFERENCE

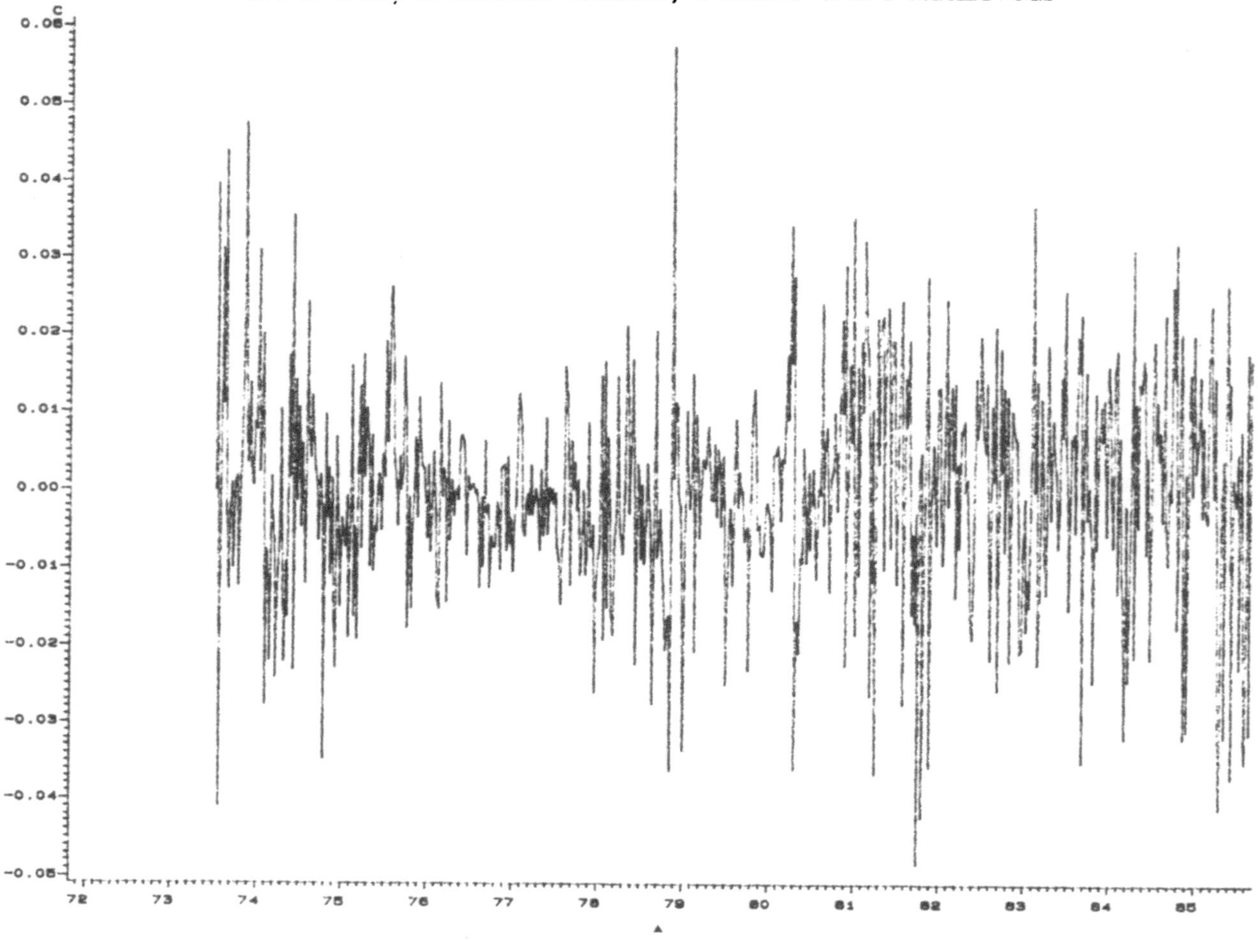

Figure 3.5

UNCONSTRAINED CONDITIONAL VARIANCE, DM

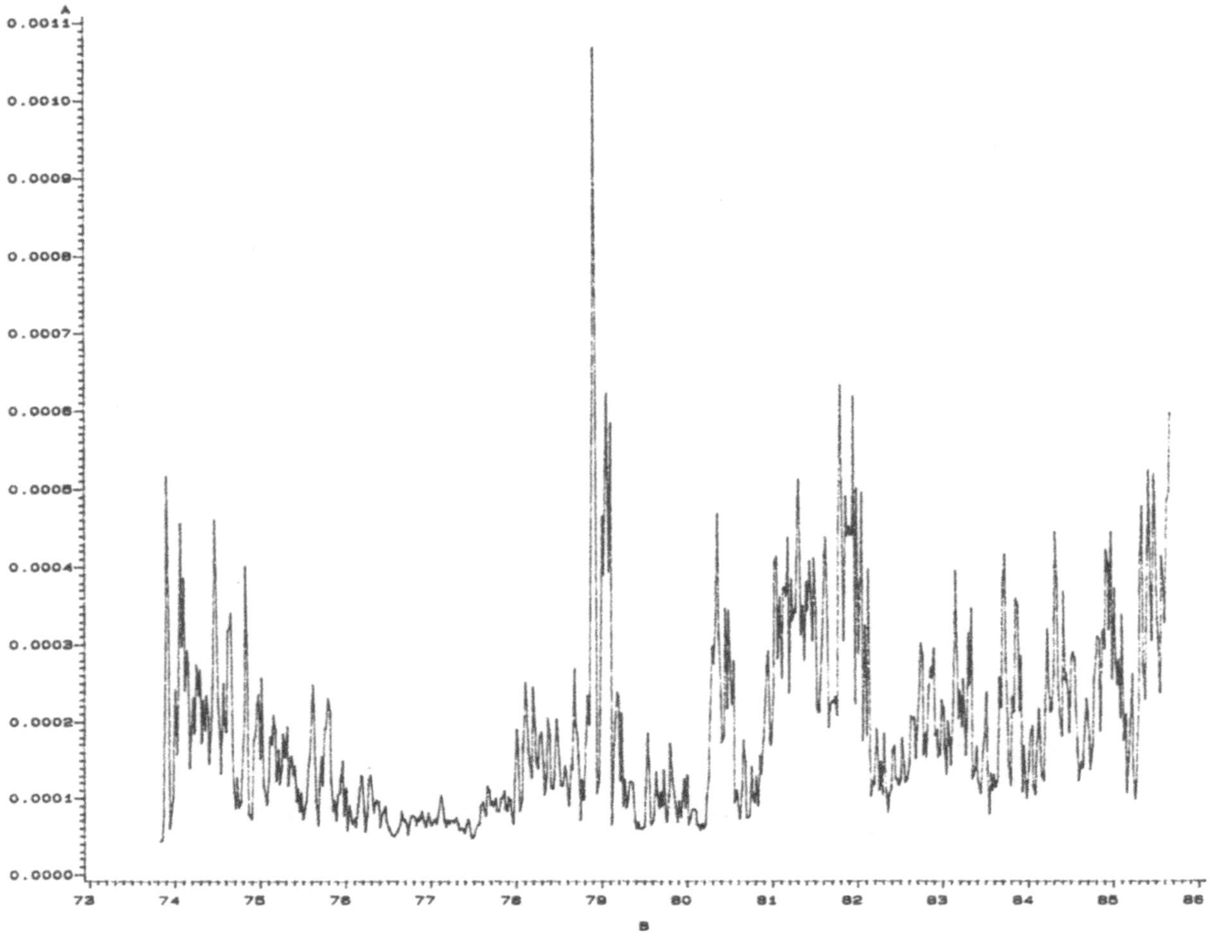

Figure 3.6

CONSTRAINED CONDITIONAL VARIANCE, DM

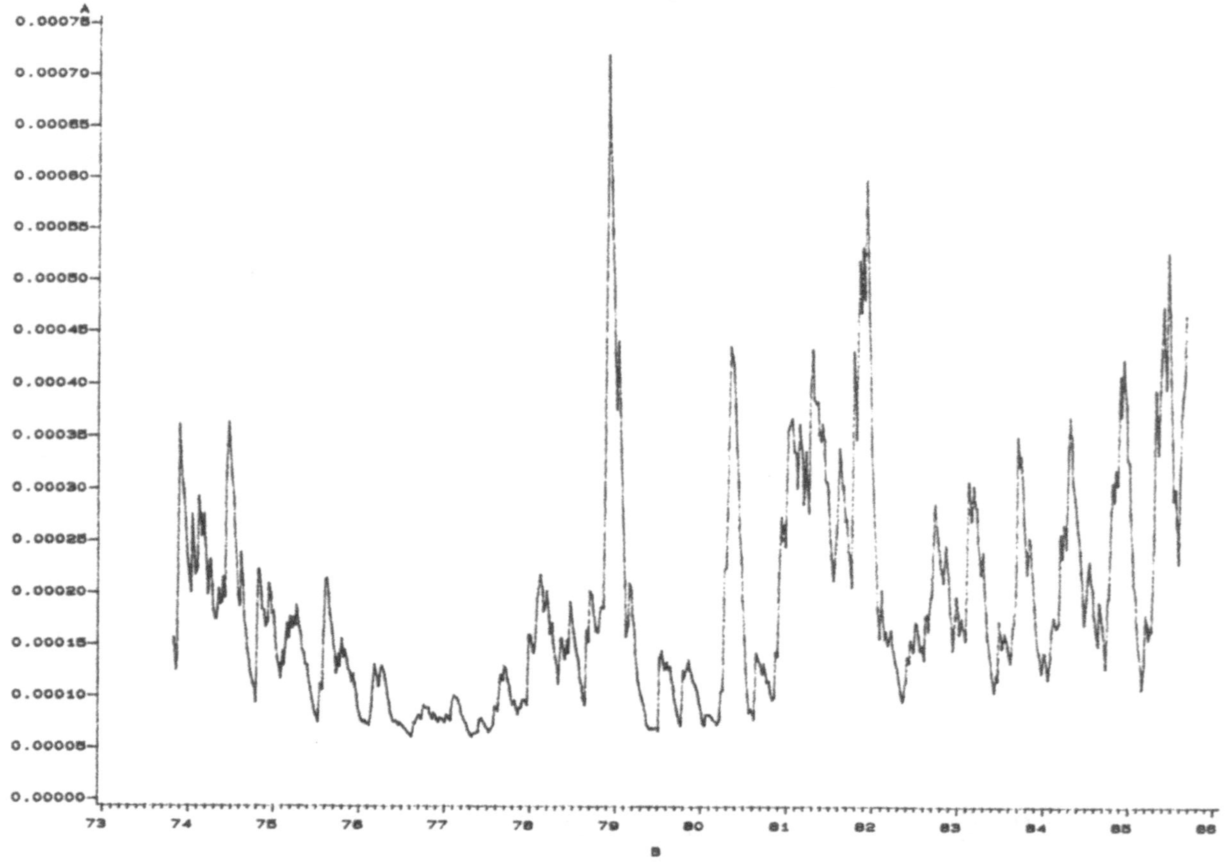

Figure 3.7
UNCONSTRAINED ARCH CONFIDENCE BANDS, DM

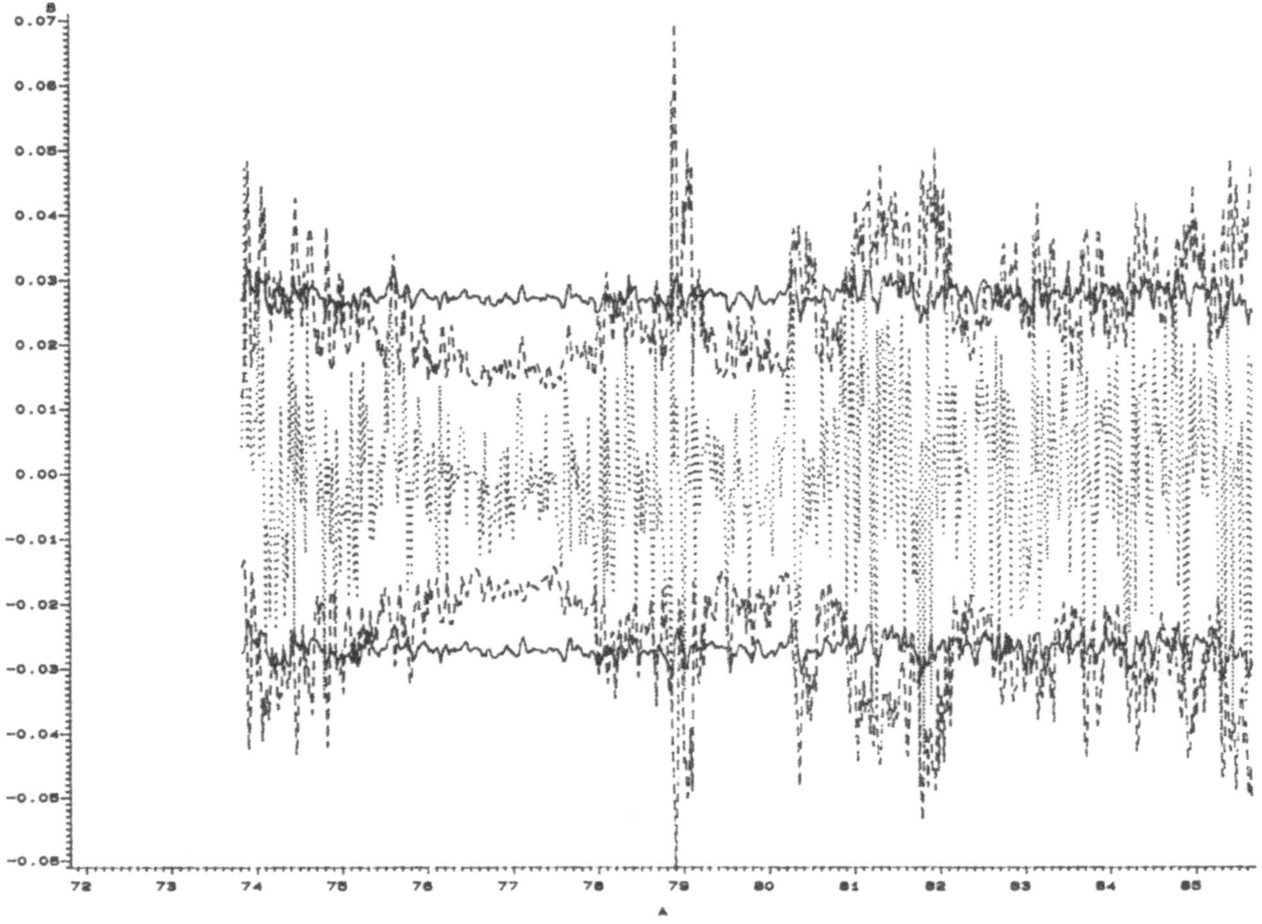

SOLID=CLASSICAL DASH=ARCH DOT=TRUE VALUE

Figure 3.8

CONSTRAINED ARCH CONFIDENCE BANDS, DM

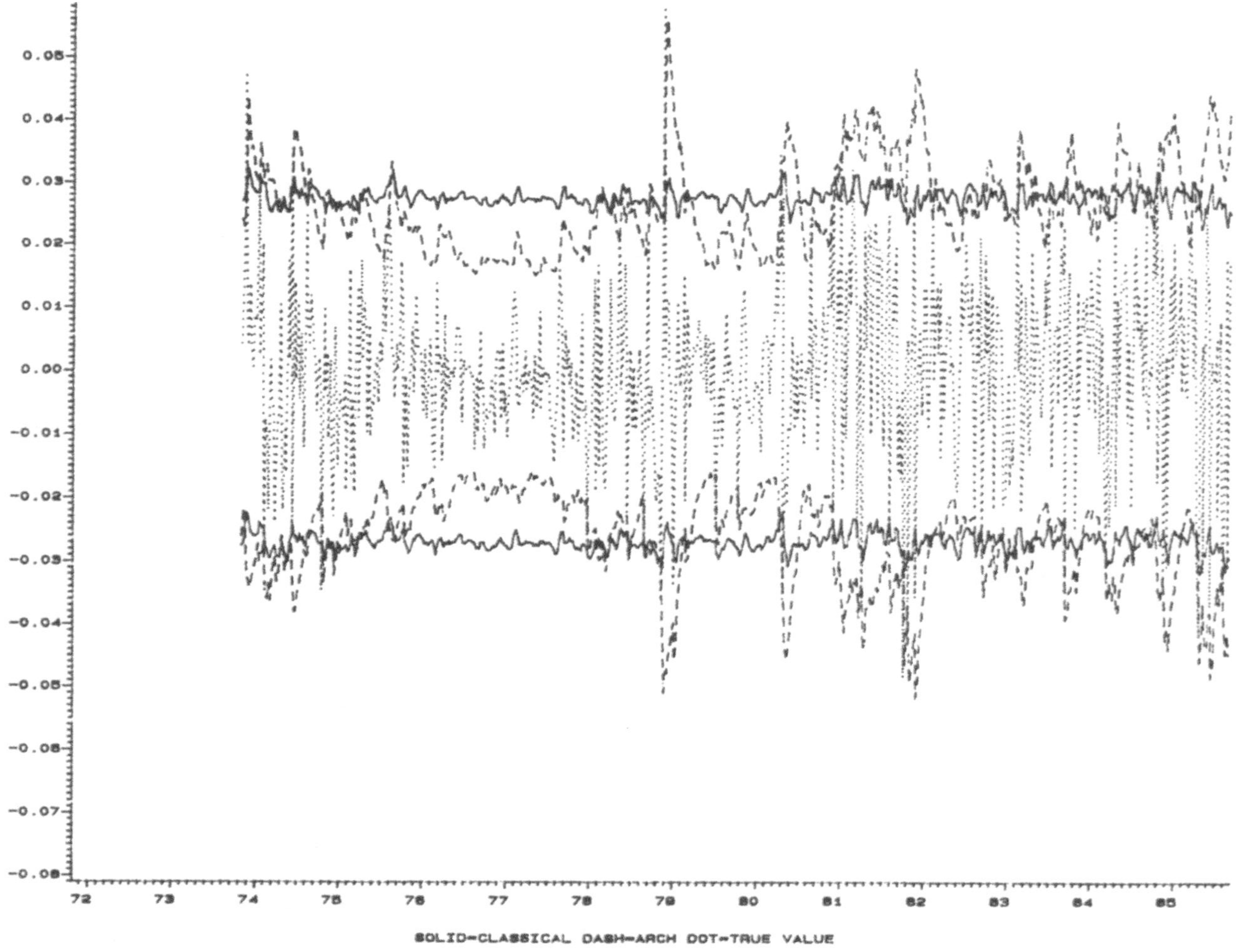

Appendix To Chapter Three: Testing For Unit Roots

A3.1) The First-Order Case

For simplicity, we consider first the problem of testing for a unit root in the first order autoregressive process. Dickey (1976) and Fuller (1976) use the Monte Carlo method to calculate the percentage points of the finite sample as well as the asymptotic distribution of $\hat{\rho}$, the least squares estimator, when $\rho = 1$. Specifically, consider the usual situation:

$$H_0: \ln S_t = \ln S_{t-1} + e_t \ , \ t = 1, 2, \ldots$$

$$H_1: \ln S_t = \rho \ln S_{t-1} + e_t$$

$$e_t \overset{iid}{\sim} N(0, \sigma^2), \ \ln S_0 = 0.$$

Consider the OLS (and ML) estimator $\hat{\rho}$ obtained from a sample of size N. Fuller (1976) shows that under H_0:

$$(\hat{\rho} - 1) = O_p(N^{-1}) \ .$$

It is interesting to note that the convergence is faster than for ρ not equal to one, in which case:

$$(\hat{\rho} - \rho) = O_p(N^{-1/2}) \ .$$

Furthermore, since:

$$(\hat{\rho} - 1) = O_p(N^{-1}) \quad \text{and } N(\hat{\rho} - 1) = O_p(1)$$

it follows that the appropriate quantity for which percentage points should be calculated under the null is $N(\hat{\rho} - 1)$.

Note that we can also make use of the usual "Student's t" for testing $\rho = 1$:

$$\hat{\tau} = \frac{\hat{\rho} - 1}{[\hat{\sigma}^2 (\sum_{t=2}^{N} \ln S_{t-1}^2)^{-1}]^{1/2}}$$

where:

$$\hat{\sigma}^2 = [1/(N-2)] \sum_{t=2}^{N} \hat{e}_t^2 = [1/(N-2)] \sum_{t=2}^{N} (\ln S_t - \hat{\rho} \ln S_{t-1})^2 .$$

Under the null, $\hat{\tau} = O_p(1)$, but it does not have the "t" distribution. Note that $\hat{\tau}$ may easily be obtained as output from a standard regression package. We have:

$$\ln S_t = \rho \ln S_{t-1} + e_t$$

or

$$\ln S_t - \ln S_{t-1} = (\rho - 1) \ln S_{t-1} + e_t .$$

Thus $\hat{\tau}$ is the usual t statistic in a regression of the first difference of $\ln S_t$ on the first lag of $\ln S_t$.

Dickey and Fuller (1979) show that $\hat{\tau}$ is a monotone function of the likelihood ratio for the null of $\rho = 1$ versus the alternative of $\rho \neq 1$. However, for more specific alternatives, like the stationary model with random initial condition, $\hat{\tau}$ is not necessarily the likelihood ratio test. Recall that the only alternative entertained thus far is:

$$\ln S_t = \rho \ln S_{t-1} + e_t \qquad t=1,2,\ldots$$

$$\ln S_0 = 0$$

$$\rho \neq 1 .$$

We could, however, refine the model to alternatives such as

$$|\rho| < 1 \text{ and } |\rho| > 1.$$

For either of these cases, a one-sided test is appropriate. Notice that if the alternative is $|\rho| < 1$ then the model is asymptotically stationary, since the effect of the fixed initial condition is transient. The $|\rho| > 1$ alternative, on the other hand, is nonstationary for all sample sizes.

Consider now the case of a nonzero mean, μ :

$$(\ln S_t - \mu) = \rho(\ln S_{t-1} - \mu) + e_t \quad t = 1, 2, \ldots$$

or

$$\ln S_t = \mu \ (1 - \rho) + \rho \ln S_{t-1} + e_t \equiv \theta + \rho \ln S_{t-1} + e_t.$$

If μ were known, we could simply center the data and proceed as before. In practice, of course, μ must be estimated along with the other parameters. Although θ vanishes under the null of $\rho = 1$, it is nevertheless present under the alternative, and so an intercept should be included in the regression. The corresponding statistics will be denoted by $\hat{\rho}_u$ and $\hat{\tau}_\mu$, and their null distribution has been tabulated.

Similarly, the alternative might include a trend:

$$(\ln S_t - a - bt) = \rho(\ln S_{t-1} - a - b(t-1)) + e_t$$

or

$$\ln S_t = a(1 - \rho) + \rho b + b(1 - \rho) t + \rho \ln S_{t-1} + e_t$$

$$\equiv \theta_1 + \theta_2 t + \rho \ln S_{t-1} + e_t.$$

Under H_0,

$$\ln S_t = b + \ln S_{t-1} + e_t,$$

but, under H_1, both the intercept and the trend enter and so they must be included in the regression. The test statistics are denoted by $\hat{\rho}_\tau$ and $\hat{\tau}_\tau$. Furthermore, Dickey and Fuller (1979) show that the null distributions of the two statistics are unaffected by the value of b. They also obtain representations for the limit distributions of all the test statistics under the null and show that they are invariant to the choice of

lnS_0. Furthermore, White (1959) has shown that the limit distributions do not depend on the normality assumption. The finite sample distributions, however, will in general depend on lnS_0, as shown by Evans and Savin (1981).

Substantial attention has been paid to the small-sample power of the $\hat{\tau}$, $\hat{\tau}_\mu$, and $\hat{\tau}_\tau$ statistics in Dickey (1984) and Dickey, Bell and Miller (1986). Clearly, inappropriate use of $\hat{\tau}_\mu$ when only $\hat{\tau}$ is needed, or use of $\hat{\tau}_\tau$ when only $\hat{\tau}_\mu$ or $\hat{\tau}$ is needed, will lead to reduced power due to the extra parameters which must be estimated. On the other hand, since we do not know whether, for example, trend might be present under the alternative, it is clearly desirable to allow for it so as not to bias the test results.

The possibility immediately arises that the large number of observations on our exchange rate series will afford us the convenience of routinely allowing for trend while simultaneously achieving high power, due to the consistency of the tests. The above-mentioned work has, however, focused only on small to medium sized samples (T = 25, 50, 100) and found substantial power differences. Consider, for example, the powers reported in Table A3.1, reprinted in modified form from Dickey, Bell and Miller (1986). The data were generated from a zero-mean AR(1) model, with $\sigma_\varepsilon^2 = 1$ and initial condition $y_0 = 0$. The tests were at the 5% level against the one-sided alternative $|\rho| < 1$, and 2000 replications were performed.

Under the null $(\rho = 1)$, the power must equal the size (.05), which is the case in the table. The typical power problem in unit root tests arises from the fact that realistic alternatives like $\rho = .7, .8, .9$ are very close to the null, making it difficult to discriminate between null and alternative. Even for N = 100 and $\rho = .9$, for example, the power of $\hat{\tau}$ is a healthy .78, while the power of $\hat{\tau}_\tau$ is only .19.

It is therefore clearly desirable to know how quickly the power of our tests increases with sample size, and in particular, how quickly the power of $\hat{\tau}_\mu$ relative to $\hat{\tau}_\tau$ approaches unity, when in fact there is no need to control for trend. We therefore extend the power study to sample sizes of N = 250, 400 and 650. The details of the Monte-Carlo procedure are exactly the same, and the results are reported in Table A3.2.

The results are of immediate interest. First, for N = 650, which is approximately the size of our exchange rate sample, the power of all test statistics increases very quickly as we move from $\rho = 1$. When $\rho = .9$, for example, the power of each test is 1.00, indicating that there is no power loss due to controlling for a nonexistent trend. Even for an extremely close alternative like $\rho = .95$, the power of $\hat{\tau}_\tau$ is a high .98. For detailed results, see Figures A3.1 to A3.8.

Second, the power of $\hat{\tau}_\tau$ relative to $\hat{\tau}_\mu$, for any fixed ρ value, first decreases and then increases as $N \rightarrow \infty$, being constrained at the right endpoint to have unit relative power, due to consistency of the tests. Similar results hold for the power of $\hat{\tau}_\mu$ relative to $\hat{\tau}$, as also shown in Figures A3.1 to A3.8.

Some elaboration is needed, as not all curves in the figures have the stated "U" shape. This is because for alternatives very close to or far from the null, we see only the left or right half of the "U," respectively. Thus, for example, the power of $\hat{\tau}_\mu$ relative to $\hat{\tau}$ appears monotone decreasing (albeit at a decreasing rate) for $\rho = .99$, and monotone increasing (at a decreasing rate) for $\rho = .8$ and $\rho = .5$, while the relative power for $\rho = .95$ and $\rho = .90$ displays the full "U" shape.

A3.2) Higher-Order Processes

Suppose an exchange rate follows the AR(p) process:

$$\ln S_t + \sum_{j=1}^{p} \alpha_j \ln S_{t-j} = e_t \quad t = p+1, p+2, \ldots .$$

We can rewrite this as:

$$\ln S_t = \theta_1 \ln S_{t-1} + \sum_{j=2}^{p} \theta_j (\ln S_{t-j+1} - \ln S_{t-j}) + e_t$$

where $p > 2$, $\theta_i = \sum_{j=i}^{p} \alpha_j$, $i=2,\ldots,p$, and $\theta_1 = - \sum_{j=1}^{p} \alpha_j$.

If there is a unit root, then $\theta_1 = 1$.

As an example, consider the AR(2) process:

$$\ln S_t + \alpha_1 \ln S_{t-1} + \alpha_2 \ln S_{t-2} = e_t, \; t = 3, 4, \ldots \quad .$$

Then,

$$\ln S_t = (-\alpha_1 - \alpha_2) \ln S_{t-1} + \alpha_2 (\ln S_{t-1} - \ln S_{t-2}) + e_t .$$

As claimed above:

$$\theta_1 = - \sum_{j=1}^{p} \alpha_j = -(\alpha_1 + \alpha_2)$$

and:

$$\theta_2 = \sum_{j=2}^{p} \alpha_j = \alpha_2 .$$

To see that $\theta_1 = 1$ corresponds to the case of a unit root, consider:

$$\ln S_t = \ln S_{t-1} + \alpha_2 (\ln S_{t-1} - \ln S_{t-2}) + e_t ,$$

which is obtained by setting $\theta_1 = 1$. Rearrangement yields:

$$(\ln S_t - \ln S_{t-1}) = \alpha_2 (\ln S_{t-1} - \ln S_{t-2}) + e_t .$$

Thus, the first difference is AR(1), which means that the original series is ARIMA(1, 1, 0), which is equivalent to an AR(2) with a unit root.

Fuller (1976) considered the distribution of $\hat{\theta}_1$ under the null of $\theta_1 = 1$ and showed that for any particular process there exists a scalar c such that $N\, c(\hat{\theta}_1 - 1)$ has the same asymptotic distribution as $\hat{\rho} \equiv N(\hat{\rho} - 1)$, the statistic for the first order case. He also shows that the studentized statistic for $\theta_1 = 1$ has the same asymptotic distribution as $\hat{\tau}$. This powerful result shows that the results for the AR(1) process generalize in a straightforward manner to higher order processes. The

$\hat{\tau}$ statistic is particularly attractive because the constant c can be difficult or impossible to determine in practice.

For the case of a nonzero mean, we have:

$$(\ln S_t - \mu) + \sum_{j=1}^{p} \alpha_j (\ln S_{t-j} - \mu) = e_t \qquad t = p+1,\ p+2, \ldots \ .$$

We can immediately put this in the form:

$$\ln S_t = K + \theta_1 \ln S_{t-1} + \sum_{j=2}^{p} \theta_j (\ln S_{t-j+1} - \ln S_{t-j}) + e_t$$

where $K = u(1 + \sum_{j=1}^{p} \alpha_j)$ and the other parameters are as above. Note that under the null of a unit root the intercept vanishes since $\sum_{j=1}^{p} \alpha_j = -1$. Fuller (1976) shows that the distribution of the "t statistic" for testing $\theta_1 = 1$ in this regression is asymptotically equivalent to that of $\hat{\tau}_u$.

Finally, consider the alternative of a linear trend:

$$(\ln S_t - a - b\ t) + \sum_{j=1}^{p} \alpha_j (\ln S_{t-j} - a - b\ (t-j)) = e_t$$

or:

$$\ln S_t = K_1 + k_2 t + \theta_1 \ln S_{t-1} + \sum_{j=2}^{p} \theta_j (\ln S_{t-j+1} - \ln S_{t-j}) + e_t$$

where:

$$K_1 = a(1 + \sum_{i=1}^{p} \alpha_i) - b \sum_{i=1}^{p} i\ \alpha_i \text{ and } K_2 = b\ (1 + \sum_{i=1}^{p} \alpha_i).$$

Thus, under the null, $K_1 = -\ b \sum_{i=1}^{p} i\ \alpha_i$ and $K_2 = 0$. Again, the asymptotic distribution of the studentized statistic is that of $\hat{\tau}_\tau$.

A3.3) General ARMA Representations

Said and Dickey (1984) extend the unit root test to the general ARMA(p,q) case by approximating the ARMA model as a finite autoregression. OLS can be used to estimate the coefficients, and this procedure produces test statistics whose limit distributions are the same as $\hat{\tau}$, $\hat{\tau}_\mu$, and $\hat{\tau}_\tau$.

Let us begin with a simple case with normal disturbances. Later we will extend the results to the general ARMA(p,q) case. Suppose:

$$\ln S_t = \rho \ln S_{t-1} + y_t \quad t = 1,2,\ldots$$

$$y_t = \alpha\, y_{t-1} + e_t + \beta\, e_{t-1} \quad t = \ldots -2,\ -1,\ 0,\ 1,\ 2,\ \ldots$$

$$|\alpha|,\ |\beta| < 1,\ \ln S_0 = 0,\ e_t \sim \text{NID} .$$

If $|\rho| < 1$, then $\ln S_t$ is stationary except for transitory startup effects. (It is an ARMA(2,1).) On the other hand, if $\rho = 1$, then it is ARIMA(1,1,1). The reader should note the following facts at the outset:

$$e_t = \sum_{j=0}^{\infty} (-\beta)^j\ (y_{t-j} - \alpha\, y_{t-j-1})$$

$$\ln S_t = \rho \ln S_{t-1} + (\alpha + \beta)\ (y_{t-1} - \beta\, y_{t-2} + \beta^2\, y_{t-3} - \ldots) + e_t .$$

We can use the above results to write:

$$\ln S_t - \ln S_{t-1} = (\rho - 1) \ln S_{t-1} + (\alpha + \beta)\ (y_{t-1} - \beta\, y_{t-2} + \beta^2\, y_{t-3} - \ldots) + e_t .$$

Under the null $y_t = \Delta \ln S_t$, so we write:

$$\Delta \ln S_t = (\alpha + \beta)\ (\Delta \ln S_{t-1} - \beta\, \Delta \ln S_{t-2} + \beta^2\, \Delta \ln S_{t-3} - \ldots) + e_t .$$

We can therefore develop a test of the null by regressing $\Delta \ln S_t$ on $\ln S_{t-1}$, $\Delta \ln S_{t-1}, \ldots, \Delta \ln S_{t-K}$, where K is a suitably chosen integer such that $N^{-1/3} K \longrightarrow 0$ (i.e. $K = o_p(N^{1/3})$). The least squares estimates of ρ, α, and β obtained by this technique are consistent under the null. However, the distribution of $N(\hat{\rho} - 1)$ depends on the unknowns α and β, so it is not useful. On the other hand, the studentized statistic $\hat{\tau}$ associated with $(\hat{\rho} - 1)$ does not involve any unknown parameters, and it therefore constitutes a useful asymptotic test.

Now, we can write the general ARMA(p+1,q) model as:

$$\ln S_t = \rho \ln S_{t-1} + y_t, \; t = 1, 2, \ldots$$

$$y_t + \sum_{i=1}^{p} \alpha_i y_{t-i} = e_t + \sum_{j=1}^{q} \beta_j e_{t-j}$$

$$\ln S_0 = 0, \; e_t \sim NID(0, \sigma^2).$$

Assume that y_t is stationary and invertible. Then we can proceed exactly as before, running:

$$\Delta \ln S_t = (\rho - 1) \ln S_{t-1} - d_1 \Delta \ln S_{t-1} - \ldots - d_K \Delta \ln S_{t-K} + e_{tK}$$

We still get the consistency results under the null, and the distribution of the t-statistic on $(\hat{\rho} - 1)$ is the same. Also, if the series mean is removed before the analysis, $\hat{\tau}_u$ should be used rather than $\hat{\tau}$.

The Dickey-Fuller-Said tests are likelihood ratio (also equivalent to Wald) tests, and they therefore require estimation under the alternative. On the other hand, an advantage of the popular Lagrange multiplier (LM) test is that it requires evaluation only under the null. (See Godfrey (1979), Breusch and Pagan (1980), and Engle (1982a).) These facts motivated Solo (1984) to develop an LM test for unit roots in the general ARMA(p,q) model:

$$\ln S_t - \phi \ln S_{t-1} - a'y_{t-1} = (1 + d(U))\, e_t(\theta)$$

where:

$$d(U) = \sum_{i=1}^{q} d_i U^i$$

$$y_{t-1} = (y_{t-1}, \ldots, y_{t-p})'$$

$$y_t = \ln S_t - \ln S_{t-1} \, .$$

Define the partitioned vector $\theta = (\phi \mid a' \mid d')$. Then the null hypothesis is that $\phi = 1$ and that there exists a "true" parameter vector θ_0 such that:

$$e_t(\theta_0) = \varepsilon_t \overset{iid}{\sim} (0, \sigma^2) \, .$$

Given a sample $(\ln S_1 \ldots \ln S_T)$, Solo derives the LM test of this hypothesis. Just as Fuller's $\hat{\tau}$ statistic is shown not to possess a limiting normal distribution, Solo's LM statistic does not possess the usual χ^2 limiting distribution. Rather, LM should have the same limiting distribution as $\hat{\tau}^2$, and Solo's proofs confirm this.

The LM test procedure amounts to the following. First, fit an ARMA(p,q) model to (y_t), and save the residuals $(\tilde{e}_t)$. Next, we generate the regressors:

$$(\tilde{\zeta}_{t-1}) = ((1 + \tilde{d}(U))^{-1} \ln S_{t-1}).$$

Finally, we regress $\tilde{e}_t$ on $\tilde{\zeta}_{t-1}$ and obtain LM as $T R^2$.

Table A3.1
Empirical Power of Unit Root Tests, 2000 Replications, One-Sided Alternative Zero-Mean AR(1) Model*

	$\hat{\tau}$	$\hat{\tau}_\mu$	$\hat{\tau}_\tau$
N = 25			
ρ = 1.00	.06	.06	.06
.99	.06	.05	.04
.98	.06	.06	.06
.95	.09	.05	.06
.90	.14	.06	.05
.80	.32	.12	.08
.50	.91	.49	.30
N = 50			
ρ = 1.00	.05	.05	.05
.99	.07	.06	.06
.98	.07	.06	.05
.95	.16	.07	.06
.90	.31	.11	.08
.80	.77	.30	.20
.50	1.00	.98	.87
N = 100			
ρ = 1.00	.04	.05	.06
.99	.08	.06	.05
.98	.12	.06	.05
.95	.31	.12	.08
.90	.78	.31	.19
.80	1.00	.86	.65
.50	1.00	1.00	1.00

* Reproduced from Dickey, Bell and Miller (1986)

Table A3.2
Empirical Power of Unit Root Tests, 2000 Replications, One-Sided Alternative
Zero-Mean AR(1) Model

N = 250

ρ	$\hat{\tau}$	$\hat{\tau}_\mu$	$\hat{\tau}_\tau$
1.00	.05	.05	.05
.99	.14	.08	.06
.97	.53	.21	.13
.95	.90	.43	.26
.90	1.00	.97	.83
.80	1.00	1.00	1.00
.50	1.00	1.00	1.00

N = 400

1.00	.05	.05	.05
.99	.23	.10	.07
.97	.87	.40	.24
.95	1.00	.85	.61
.90	1.00	1.00	1.00
.80	1.00	1.00	1.00
.50	1.00	1.00	1.00

N = 650

1.00	.05	.05	.05
.99	.43	.16	.10
.97	1.00	.83	.58
.95	1.00	1.00	.98
.90	1.00	1.00	1.00
.80	1.00	1.00	1.00
.50	1.00	1.00	1.00

Figure A.3.1

POWER CURVES, N = 25

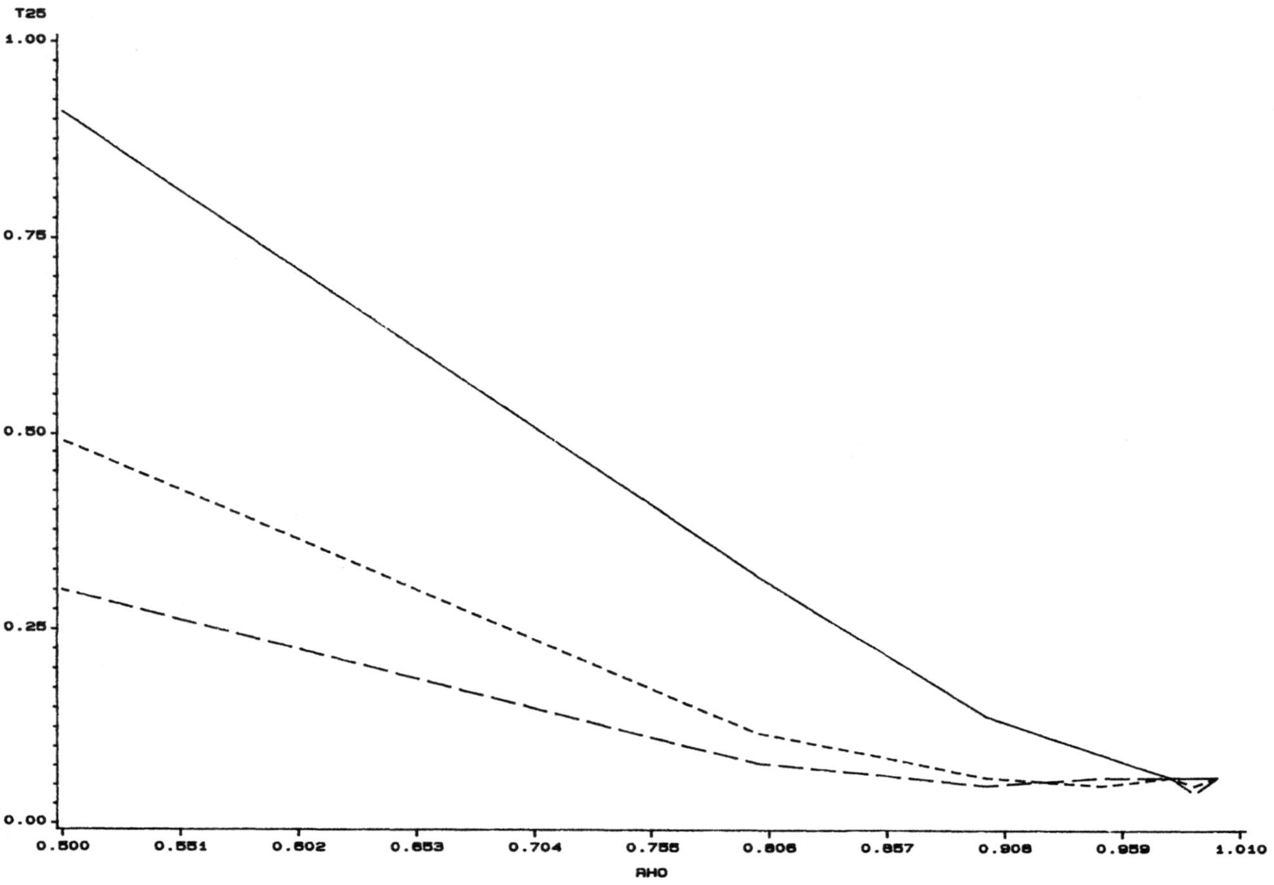

T = SOLID, TU = DASH, TT = DOT

Figure A.3.2

POWER CURVES, N = 50

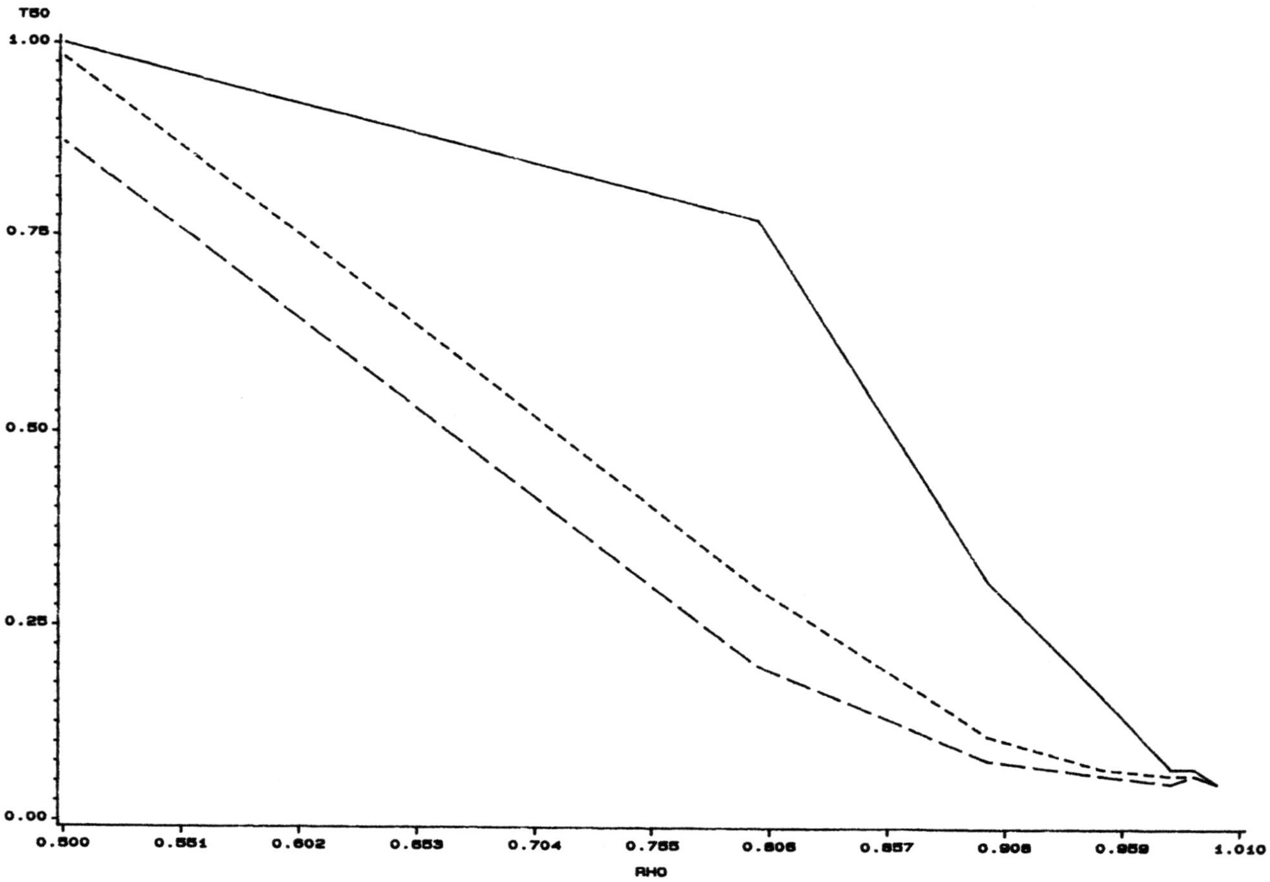

T = SOLID, TU = DASH, TT = DOT

Figure A.3.3

POWER CURVES, N = 100

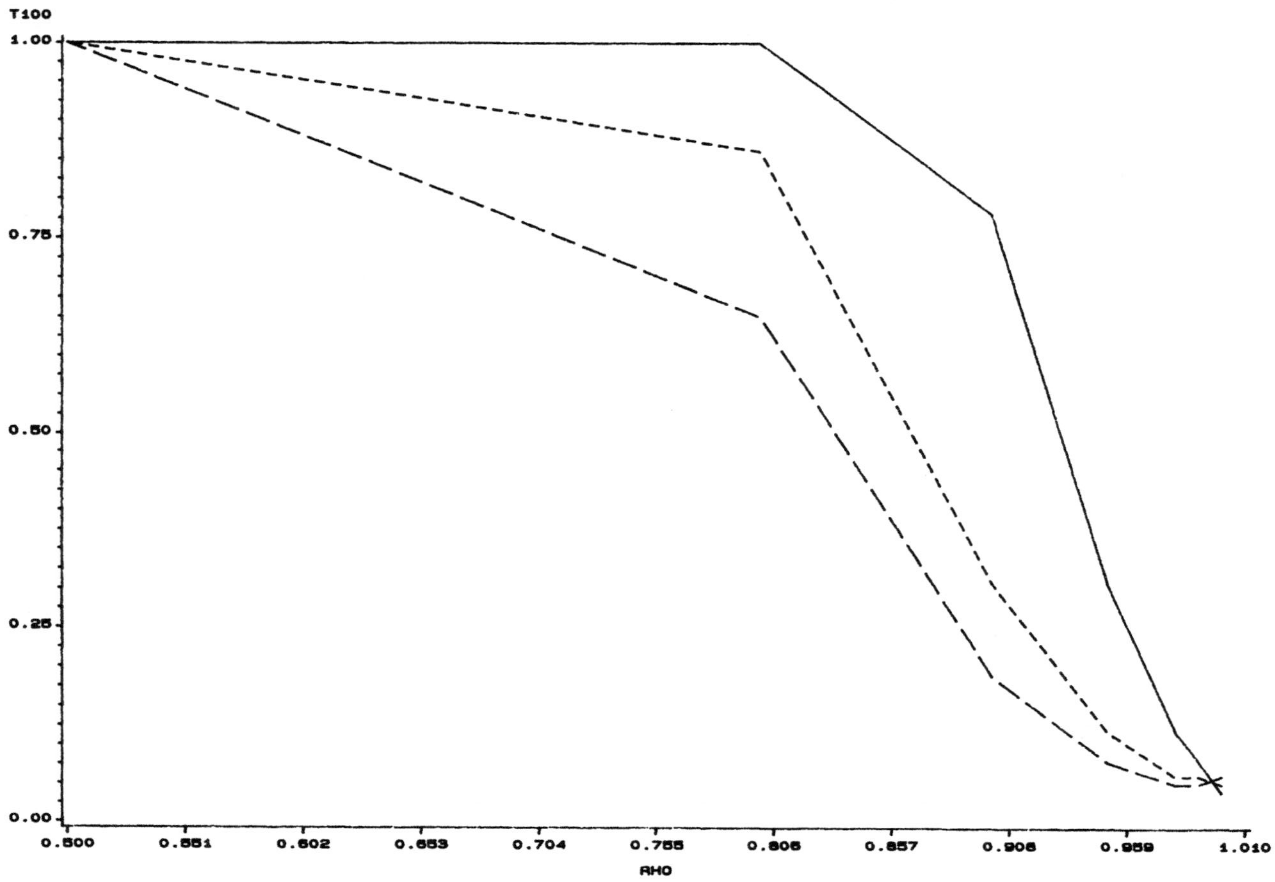

T = SOLID, TU = DASH, TT = DOT

Figure A.3.4

POWER CURVES, N = 250

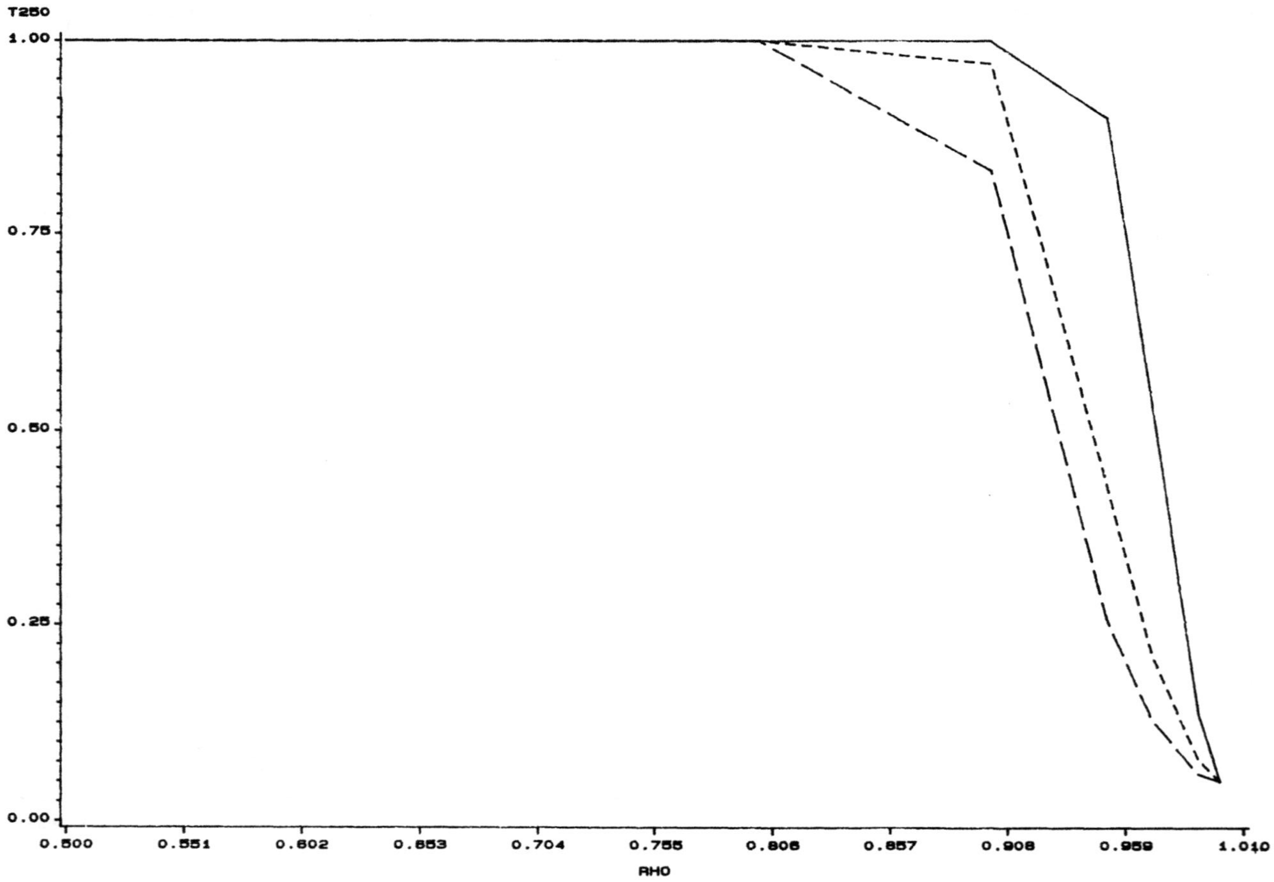

T = SOLID, TU = DASH, TT = DOT

Figure A.3.5

POWER CURVES, N = 400

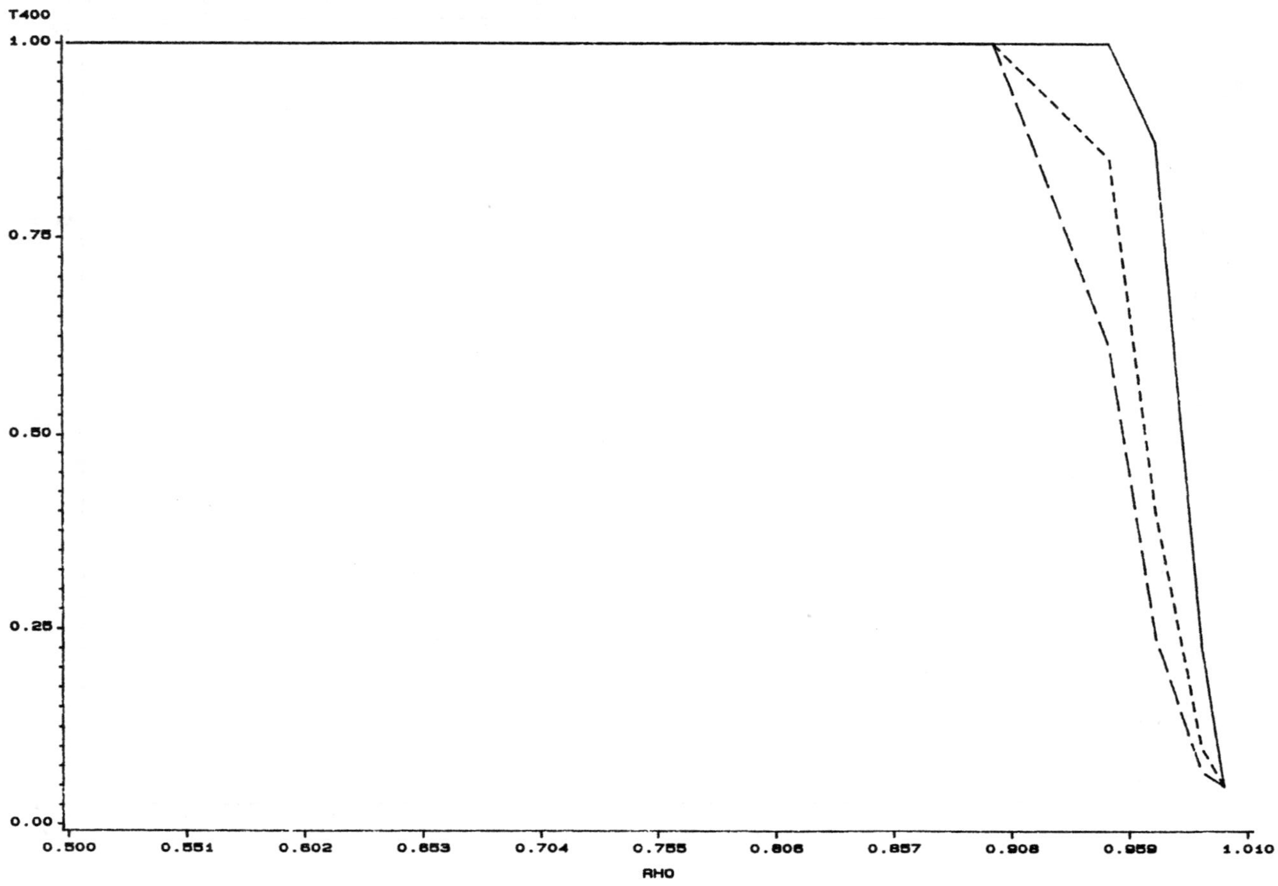

T = SOLID, TU = DASH, TT = DOT

Figure A.3.6

POWER CURVES, N = 650

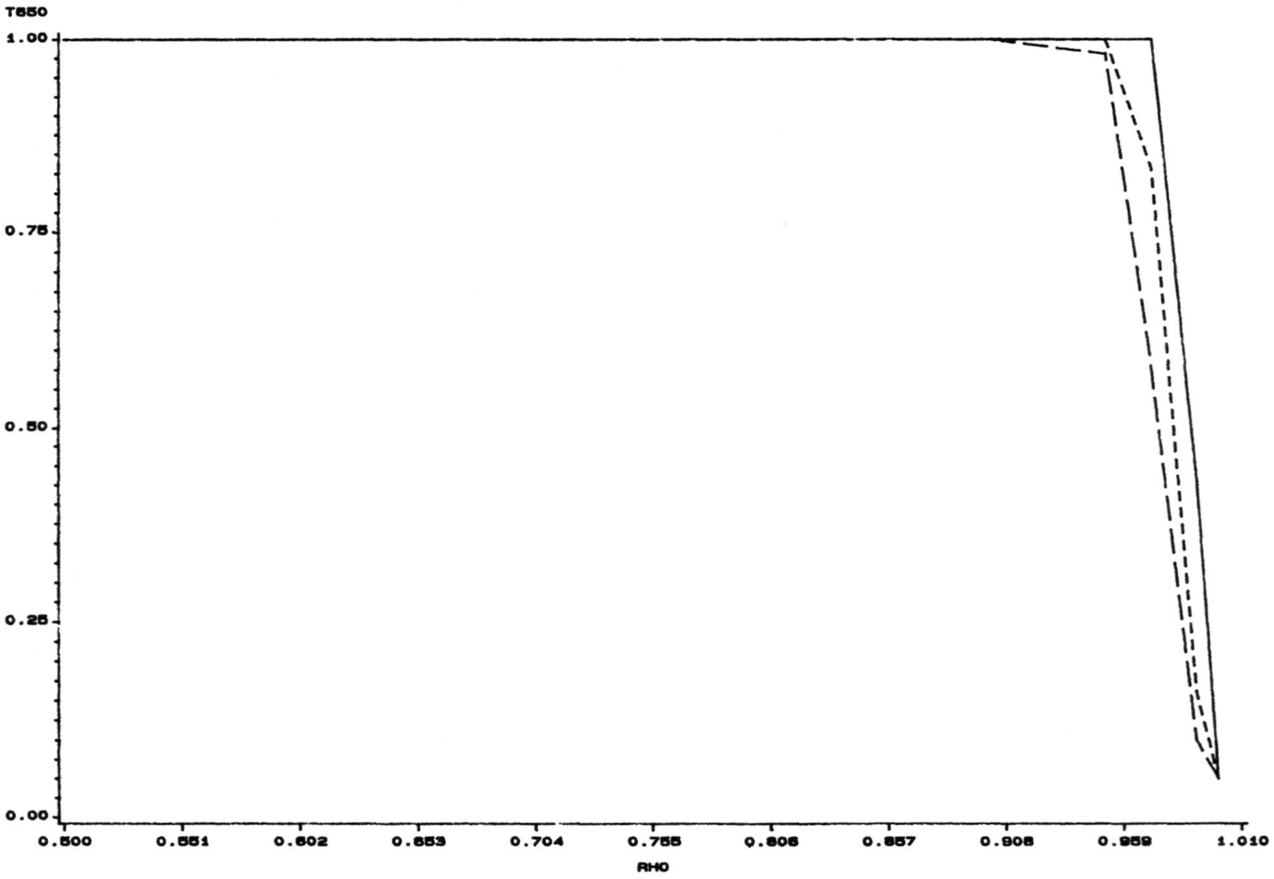

T = SOLID, TU = DASH, TT = DOT

Figure A.3.7

POWER OF TT RELATIVE TO TU

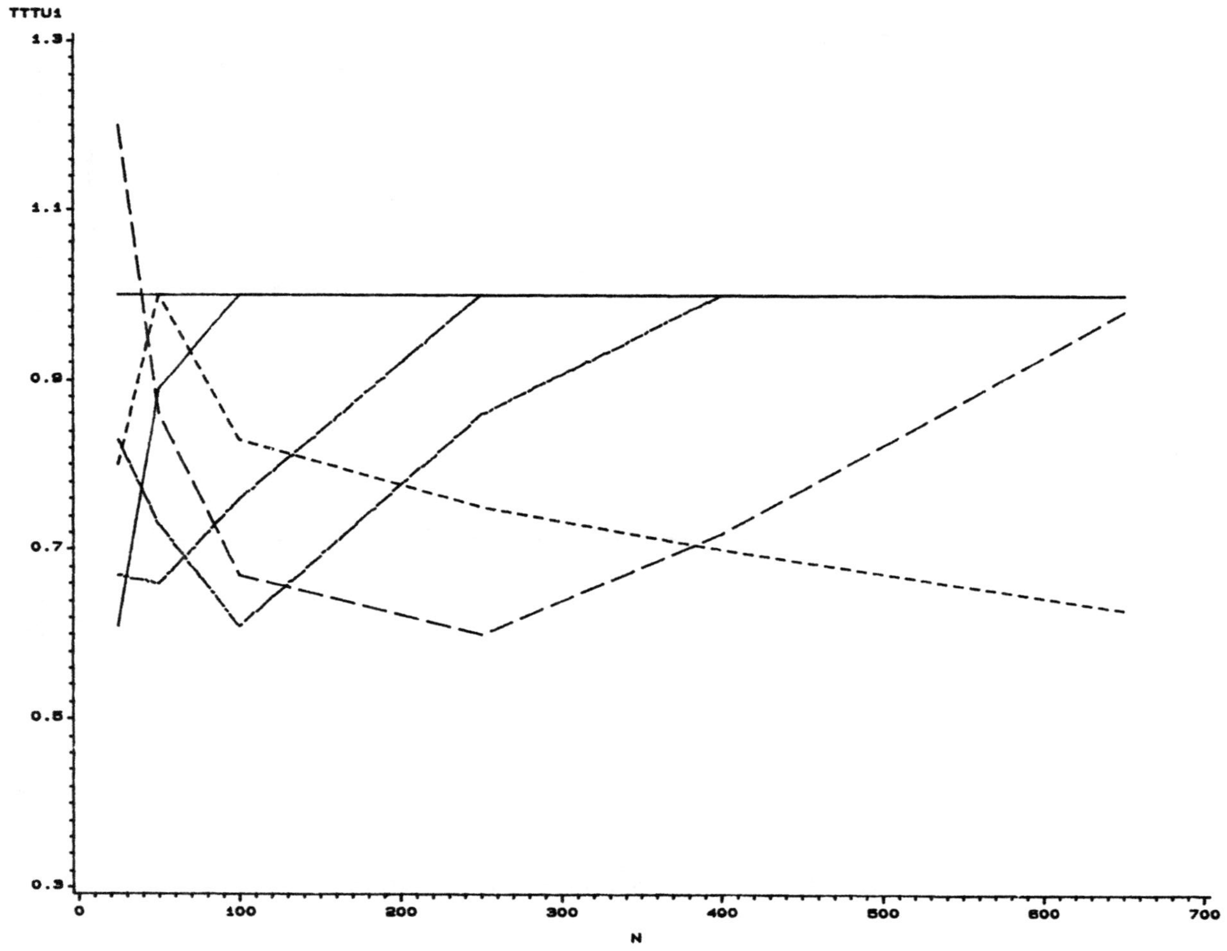

Figure A.3.8

POWER OF TU RELATIVE TO T

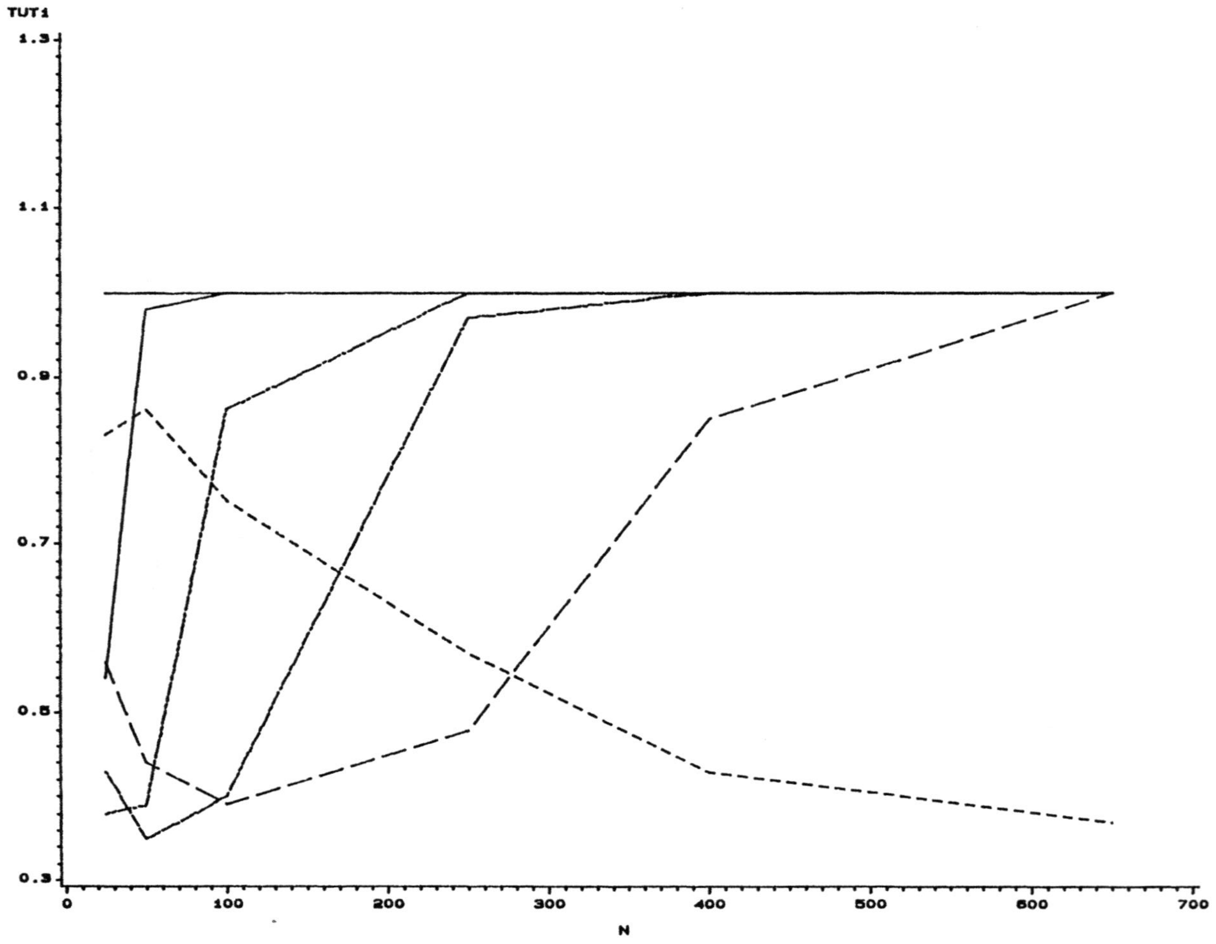

Chapter Four: Monthly Univariate Nominal Exchange Rate Fluctuations

4.1) Introduction

We have seen in Chapter 3 that high frequency nominal dollar spot rates are well described by approximate random walks whose innovations display substantial autoregressive conditional heteroskedasticity. It was shown that this fact explains the Meese-Rogoff finding that simple random walks dominate a wide variety of structural models in terms of predictive ability, enables measurement of the temporal behavior of exchange rate volatility, explains the leptokurtic unconditional distribution of exchange rate movements, and enables improved calculation of confidence intervals about point forecasts.

In this chapter we study the same nominal dollar spot rates measured at monthly, rather than weekly, frequency. Particular attention is paid to the nature of any serial correlation present in both the conditional mean and conditional variance, in light of the theoretical results on temporal aggregation of ARCH processes given in Chapter 2.

The extension to monthly data is important because it enables us to ascertain how much, if at all, the strong conditional heteroskedasticity present at the weekly frequency is reduced when we move to monthly data. In one sense, then, the monthly analysis provides a direct check on our theoretical results, which indicate that both the ARCH effects and the leptokurtosis should be reduced in monthly data. The theory provides little guidance, however, as to how quickly these phenomena will be reduced; the monthly analysis is therefore useful because it enables us to take a direct look.

In addition, the monthly frequency is typically the highest at which structural exchange rate models can be estimated, due to problems of data availability. A finding of conditional heteroskedasticity in the monthly time-series has implications for structural estimation and prediction, because if it is not eliminated by controlling for exogenous variables, then efficient parameter estimation and prediction interval calculation require controlling for it. In this sense the study of monthly nominal spot rates is a necessary prerequisite to the study of real exchange rates and purchasing power parity in Chapter 5.

4.2) Empirical Analysis

We use end-of-month nominal spot rate data for the same period as in the weekly analysis, July 1973 through August 1985, which yields 146 observations. As before, all exchange rates are measured in local currency units per dollar, with the exception of the BP, for which the opposite is true. Strong nonstationarity in all rates is once again evident. The sample autocorrelations and partial autocorrelations, shown in Tables 4.1 and 4.2 respectively, again indicate conditional mean behavior very close to that of a random walk. This is formally verified by the unit root tests allowing for nonzero mean and trend reported in Tables 4.3 and 4.4. In no case can we reject the null of one unit root at any reasonable significance level; joint tests, however, sharply reject the null of two unit roots. As before, it should be kept in mind that the tests are robust to conditional heteroskedasticity.

The finding of approximate random walk conditional mean behavior at the monthly frequency is to be expected, due to the well-known result that n-period temporal aggregation of a random walk process with unconditional innovation variance σ^2 yields another random walk process with innovation variance $n\,\sigma^2$.[1] More generally, temporal aggregation of an ARMA process with d unit roots yields another ARMA process with d unit roots.[2]

The first-differenced series contain a number of interesting features. First, the amplitude of $\Delta \ln S$ is substantially larger in the case of monthly observations. This is due to the earlier-mentioned increase of innovation variance due to temporal aggregation. Second, although there does appear to be some volatility clustering, it

---

This restriction will be examined in detail subsequently.
See Brewer (1973) and Amemiya and Wu (1972).

is certainly not as pronounced as in the weekly case. Third, the amplitude of extreme values relative to average fluctuation amplitude appears less, which should lead to reduced kurtosis. This phenomenon is, of course, intimately linked to the decreased volatility clustering, a subject to which we shall return.

The sample autocorrelations and Bartlett standard errors of $\Delta \ln S$ are given in Table 4.5, in which we see no evidence of serial correlation. This should be contrasted with the corresponding table of Chapter 3, in which we saw that the weekly data did display some evidence of weak serial correlation, particularly at short lags. This is to be expected, since temporal aggregation reduces serial dependence.

This decreased serial dependence is also reflected in the Ljung-Box statistics reported in Table 4.6. As opposed to the weekly series, five out of seven of which displayed some evidence of serial correlation (particularly at low lags) now there is only one questionable series, the CD. Further examination indicates, however, that the "significance" of LB(12) and LB(18) in the case of the CD is largely spurious, arising from the sample autocorrelations at lags 11 and 12. We can only attribute this phenomenon to type-I error, there being little evidence of seasonality in the series and strong theoretical reasons against seasonality.[3] The absence of serial correlation is confirmed in the frequency domain by Fisher's kappa, which, like the LB statistics, appears significant only for the CD.

Some evidence of nonzero mean in first-differenced form is shown for the CD, FF, and LIR, just as in the weekly case. Again, this is expected, because those three series are best described as integrated deviations from trend.

The sample skewness and kurtosis are of great interest. Skewness is little changed from the weekly analysis, being very close to zero. The kurtosis (again scaled such that a kurtosis of zero corresponds to normality) is drastically reduced, however. The kurtoses of the CD, FF, LIR, YEN, and BP are all substantially lower, the average reduction being 2.52. The kurtoses of the DM and SF are very slightly

---

[3] Seasonal effects would typically lead to significant and positive autocorrelations at seasonal lags (multiples of 12). Instead, we have a significant negative lag-12 sample autocorrelation and insignificant sample autocorrelations at all other seasonal lags. We conclude that there is really no case for seasonality and attribute the result to type I error.

increased, with an average increase of .26, probably due to sampling fluctuations. Overall, the average kurtosis reduction is a healthy 1.73. It should be noted, however, that while the monthly data are substantially closer to normality than the weekly data, we have still not obtained complete convergence to normality. Average monthly kurtosis is 1.78, as opposed to an average weekly kurtosis of 3.52.

The remaining nonnormality is clearly indicated in the reported values of the Kolmogorov D, Kiefer-Salmon, and studentized range statistics. While the values of the test statistics are typically much smaller than those of their weekly counterparts, we nevertheless tend to reject normality for most series at most significance levels. The bulk of the nonnormality is due to leptokurtosis, as evidenced by the KS2 statistics, all of which lead to rejection at the 1% level.

The sample variances of Table 4.6 are of independent interest. It was mentioned earlier that temporal aggregation of a random walk process leads to another random walk process with larger innovation variance:

$$\sigma_*^2 = n\,\sigma^2 .$$

Comparison of Tables 4.6 and 3.8 reveals that the monthly innovation variance is indeed substantially larger for the monthly series. The ratio of monthly to weekly innovation variances for the CD, FF, DM, LIR, YEN, SF and BP are, respectively, 5.67, 5.63, 5.84, 5.38, 6.38, 8.94, and 3.85. It is of interest to note that most of the variance ratios are greater than five. This is somewhat larger than expected, because the monthly/weekly variance ratio for a pure random walk should be between four and five.

The results of the Lagrange multiplier test for autoregressive conditional heteroskedasticity are contained in Table 4.7, in which we see that there is substantial evidence of ARCH, but not to the same extent as in the weekly case. Again, this is consistent with our theoretical results on temporal aggregation of ARCH processes, which indicate convergence to normality, and hence no ARCH. The CD, FF, and SF now display little evidence of ARCH, while the other series display smaller ARCH effects than in the weekly case. Even for those series which still display significant

ARCH effects, there is a noticeable reduction in order; the TR^2 statistics and the linear regressions which produced them indicated that ARCH(4) models were more than adequate for the innovations in each exchange rate.

4.3) Comparison With Some Well-Known Results From Finance

The results of this chapter, as well as those of Chapters 2 and 3, are intimately related to, and have implications for, a huge body of literature in finance. Because the important capital asset pricing model of Sharpe (1964) and Lintner (1965) assumes iid normal security returns, the assumption has been subjected to extensive empirical testing. The normality assumption has its roots in the work of Bachelier (1900), who developed a model in which asset price changes at any "low enough" frequency (weekly, monthly, etc.) are approximately normal, by assuming that asset price changes from transaction to transaction are independently, identically distributed from a density $f(\Delta P)$ such that $var(\Delta P) < \infty$.[4] Then, by the Lindberg-Levy central limit theorem, the lower frequency price changes, being the sum of a very large number of high-frequency transaction price changes, are approximately normal.

However, daily and weekly stock return data do not confirm this prediction; they are approximately symmetric but nevertheless highly leptokurtic. This fact, together with the realization that more general central limit theorems (not requiring $var(\Delta P) < \infty$) guarantee only convergence to the stable Paretian family, has led modern researchers to the use of symmetric stable distributions for return-generating processes. This is the motivating force behind the seminal work of Mandelbrot (1963), Fama (1965), and Fama and Roll (1968,1971), for example.

A number of problems remain, however. First, as pointed out by Fama (1976), although most financial models can be developed under the assumption of symmetric stable returns, the statistical tools for handling them are either poorly developed or

4 He also implicitly assumed that transactions are uniformly spaced across time, to avoid subordination effects. See Clark (1973).

completely nonexistent.[5] Second, the symmetric stable family is actually quite restrictive in the sense that there is only one member (the normal distribution, corresponding to $\alpha = 2$) which has finite variance. All other members ($0 < \alpha < 2$) have infinite variance. Third, a substantial amount of recent evidence, such as Martin and Klemosky (1975), Bey and Pinches (1980), Giacotto and Ali (1982,1985), Barone-Adesi and Talwar (1983), and Diebold, Lee and Im (1985), indicates that the iid assumption may be seriously violated due to the systematic presence of heteroskedasticity. Thus, more general central limit theorems are needed. Finally, the fact that asset price or return data approach normality when aggregated (from daily to weekly to monthly, for example) contradicts the stable Paretian models. The standard response to this problem has been to ignore it, using data sufficiently aggregated such that the assumption of normality is roughly justified.

The ARCH model, together with the limiting results of chapter 2, represents a powerful alternative to the stable Paretian models. While stock returns are not the subject of this monograph, the analysis of foreign exchange "returns" is analogous. In fact, a common stochastic representation for nominal log spot exchange rate changes, as pioneered by Westerfield (1977), is stable Paretian. Westerfield studies five weekly exchange rates over the fixed rate period 1962-1971, and the very early part of the float, 1973-1975. She finds that the normal distribution is generally rejected in favor of a Paretian distribution with characteristic exponent less than 2.0, and that exchange rate "volatility" is greater under the float. The ARCH model allows us to

---

[5] In fact, only two explicit densities of the (uncountably infinitely) many members of the symmetric stable family have been obtained. The family is therefore defined in terms of its characteristic function $\phi(t)$. A random variable X is said to be symmetric stable if:

$$\ln \phi_x(t) = a\ i\ t - c\ |t|^{\alpha}$$

where a is the origin, $c^{1/\alpha}$ is a scale parameter, and α is the characteristic exponent.

If $(\alpha, a, c) = (2, 0, 1/2\ \sigma^2)$, we have a normal distribution, and if $(\alpha, a, c) = (1, 0, 1)$, we get the Cauchy distribution. No other symmetric stable distribution has a known elementary form. See Kendall and Stuart (1977), p. 122-123.

examine volatility movements within regimes, as opposed to simply documenting obvious movements across regimes. Furthermore, by broadening the admissible class of finite-variance unconditional densities, ARCH models usually identify finite variance parameterizations.

4.4) Concluding Remarks

We find that monthly nominal log dollar spot exchange rates, while fat-tailed, are much closer to normality than their weekly counterparts; furthermore, ARCH effects are still present but are considerably reduced. This directly supports the predictions of chapter 2, in which central limit theorems for ARCH processes were proved.

The near-random walk models with ARCH effects which we have identified differ in a crucial aspect from the iid stable Paretian models in the literature: successive observations, while uncorrelated, are not independent. This not only produces better models in terms of descriptive accuracy (including convergence to normality under temporal aggregation) and interval prediction, but also provides a key link between studies of exchange rate distributional properties and studies of exchange rate volatility.

Table 4.1
Monthly Nominal Dollar Spot Rates
Sample Autocorrelations of lnS

Lag	CD	FF	DM	LIR	YEN	SF	BP
1	.975	.978	.973	.979	.969	.975	.973
2	.953	.961	.947	.956	.934	.946	.947
3	.933	.937	.913	.930	.903	.912	.914
4	.909	.911	.878	.904	.866	.877	.881
5	.884	.884	.844	.878	.825	.840	.847
6	.858	.857	.812	.854	.782	.803	.810
7	.830	.830	.779	.829	.742	.768	.769
8	.807	.803	.746	.805	.704	.734	.727
9	.782	.776	.711	.779	.662	.705	.685
10	.757	.749	.679	.754	.622	.677	.643
11	.733	.722	.643	.729	.586	.649	.600
12	.704	.695	.607	.703	.547	.618	.556

Table 4.2
Monthly Nominal Dollar Spot Rates
Sample Partial Autocorrelations of lnS

Lag	CD	FF	DM	LIR	YEN	SF	BP
1	.975	.980	.973	.979	.969	.975	.973
2	.042	.038	.007	-.042	-.068	-.099	.004
3	.031	-.160	-.169	-.072	.052	-.099	-.143
4	-.096	-.064	-.030	-.027	-.134	-.051	-.031
5	-.024	-.019	.030	.027	-.066	-.032	-.020
6	-.054	.004	-.007	-.033	-.057	-.010	-.066
7	-.034	-.024	-.035	-.006	.038	.025	-.114
8	.066	-.013	-.014	.002	-.005	.010	-.016
9	-.029	-.022	-.051	-.051	-.068	.046	.001
10	-.018	.002	.014	-.007	.019	.002	-.042
11	-.016	-.007	-.054	.003	.011	-.041	-.031
12	-.075	-.031	-.061	-.019	-.069	-.082	-.049

Table 4.3
Monthly Nominal Dollar Spot Rates
Test For Unit Root in lnS, Nonzero Mean Allowed Under The Alternative

$\Delta \ln S$	const	$\ln S_{-1}$	$\Delta \ln S_{-1}$	$\Delta \ln S_{-2}$	$\Delta \ln S_{-3}$	$\Delta \ln S_{-4}$	$\Delta \ln S_{-5}$
CD	.00282 (1.53)	-.00373 (-.32)	-.11108 (-1.28)	-.17258 (-1.97)**	.11417 (1.29)	.03739 (.43)	.09516 (1.09)
FF	.01147 (.62)	-.00534 (-.49)	-.09284 (1.08)	.11029 (1.25)	.06930 (.78)	.12241 (1.37)	.09118 (1.03)
DM	.01931 (1.18)	-.02258 (-1.18)	-.02447 (-.28)	.11131 (1.26)	.00038 (.00)	-.03368 (-.38)	.00661 (.08)
LIR	.01439 (.28)	-.00105 (-.14)	-.01794 (-.21)	.11439 (1.32)	.03994 (.46)	-.08887 (-1.02)	.05667 (.65)
YEN	.22690 (1.90)*	-.04132 (-1.91)	.06826 (.79)	-.04587 (-.53)	.14042 (1.64)*	.05142 (.60)	.05794 (.67)
SF	.02655 (1.94)*	-.03719 (-2.17)	.03348 (.39)	.10925 (1.24)	.02821 (.32)	-.01035 (-.12)	-.00640 (-.07)
BP	.00841 (.88)	-.01725 (-1.20)	.03898 (.45)	.13100 (1.47)	-.06870 (-.77)	.06332 (.71)	.13749 (1.54)

* Significant at 10% Level
** Significant at 5% Level
*** Significant at 2% Level

Table 4.4
Monthly Nominal Dollar Spot Rates
Test For Unit Root in lnS, Trend Allowed Under The Alternative

$\Delta\ln S$	const	t	$\ln S_{-1}$	$\Delta\ln S_{-1}$	$\Delta\ln S_{-2}$	$\Delta\ln S_{-3}$	$\Delta\ln S_{-4}$	$\Delta\ln S_{-5}$
CD	-.00768 (-1.98)**	.00033 (3.06)***	-.13479 (-3.04)	-.04344 (-.49)	-.11136 (-1.28)	.16746 (1.91)*	.08815 (1.02)	.14244 (1.66)*
FF	.04012 (1.77)*	.00024 (2.11)**	-.03376 (-1.96)	-.09263 (-1.09)	.11056 (1.26)	.07197 (.82)	.12539 (1.42)	.09964 (1.14)
DM	.01341 (.80)	.00012 (1.66)*	-.02716 (-1.41)	-.03770 (-.44)	.09725 (1.11)	-.01232 (-.14)	-.04937 (-.56)	-.00633 (-.07)
LIR	.24657 (1.75)*	.00034 (1.76)*	-.03876 (-1.71)	-.00215 (-.02)	.13052 (1.51)	.05947 (.68)	-.06731 (-.77)	.07403 (.85)
YEN	.31883 (2.12)**	-.00008 (-1.01)	-.05674 (-2.14)	.07646 (.89)	-.03652 (-.42)	.15095 (1.75)*	.06214 (.71)	.06926 (.79)
SF	.01519 (.78)	.00008 (.82)	-.03071 (-1.63)	.02308 (.27)	.09575 (1.07)	.01489 (.17)	-.02455 (-.27)	-.02025 (-.23)
BP	.03215 (1.64)*	-.00013 (-1.38)	-.03744 (-1.83)	.04692 (.55)	.13916 (1.57)	-.06069 (-.68)	.07134 (.80)	.14691 (1.64)*

* Significant at 10% Level
** Significant at 5% Level
*** Significant at 2% Level

Table 4.5
Monthly Nominal Dollar Spot Rates
Sample Autocorrelations and Barlett Standard Errors, $\Delta \ln S$

Lag	CD	FF	DM	LIR	YEN	SF	BP
1	-.105 (.083)-->	-.075	-.027	-.022	.049	.042	.030
2	-.167 (.084)-->	.102	.082	.095	-.052	.100	.109
3	.128 (.086)-->	.043	-.005	.024	.114	.023	-.052
4	.026 (.088)-->	.110	-.030	-.080	.046	-.009	.055
5	.044 (.088)-->	.067	-.010	.064	.023	-.021	.101
6	-.089 (.088)-->	-.059	-.071	-.020	-.070	-.089	-.035
7	-.077 (.088)-->	.007	.040	.030	-.008	.031	.018
8	.110 (.089)-->	.011	.047	.048	.071	-.043	-.050
9	-.070 (.090)-->	-.001	-.026	-.002	-.057	-.010	.056
10	-.009 (.090)-->	.016	.074	.005	-.061	-.019	.048
11	.195* (.090)-->	.003	.031	-.032	.050	.060	.102
12	-.226* (.093)-->	-.066	-.094	-.073	.082	-.027	-.061

*exceeds two standard errors

Table 4.6
Monthly Nominal Dollar Spot Rates
Test Statistics, ΔlnS

	CD	FF	DM	LIR	YEN	SF	BP
LB(6)	9.85	5.70	2.03	3.17	3.88	3.16	4.52
LB(12)	27.68***	6.47	5.15	4.69	7.25	4.36	8.05
LB(18)	34.90**	8.88	8.26	5.85	17.02	9.81	19.55
M-1	72	72	72	72	72	72	72
MaxP	.003	.006	.008	.006	.008	.008	.010
SumP	.025	.155	.159	.124	.147	.207	.150
FK	7.6731**	2.9794	3.5676	3.3169	3.8604	2.9444	4.8123
Mean	.00214	.00498	.00116	.00801	-.00072	-.00157	-.00403
t(μ=0)	1.96**	1.83*	.41900	3.28***	-.27	-.50	-1.50
Variance	.00017	.00107	.00111	.00086	.00102	.00143	.00104
Std. Dev.	.01317	.03278	.03327	.02933	.03196	.03788	.03232
CV	614.816	658.063	2873.9	366.314	-4416.68	-2410.93	-801.094
Skewness	.92183	.08977	-.09614	.46747	-.29676	.13758	.69625
Kurtosis	3.52449	1.35460	1.37567	1.10453	1.50095	1.86460	1.80866
D	.12414***	.08386**	.07643**	.09759***	.12505***	.07866**	.06414
KS	103.40***	9.76***	9.98***	13.93***	14.50***	18.55***	21.58***
KS1	18.23***	.15	.22	3.46**	2.08	.45	11.08***
KS2	85.17***	9.61***	9.76***	10.47***	12.42***	18.11***	10.50***
Maximum	.06260	.11117	.10211	.09424	.11525	.15475	.13135
Q3	.00766	.02356	.02184	.02223	.01648	.02084	.01267
Median	.00166	.00344	.00087	.00487	.00184	-.00029	-.00498
Q1	-.00592	-.01076	-.01510	-.00677	-.01180	-.02230	-.02435
Minimum	-.02943	-.09183	-.10998	-.06721	-.09132	-.11642	-.07912
SR	6.98785***	6.19216*	6.37481**	5.50460	6.46339**	7.15866***	6.51207**

NOTES: LB(N) = Ljung-Box statistic at lag N
M-1 = number of independent periodogram ordinates
MaxP = maximum periodogram ordinate, MinP = minimum periodogram ordinate
SumP = sum of periodogram ordinates
FK = Fisher's kappa
CV = coefficient of variation
D = Kolmogorov's D for the null hypothesis of normality
KS = Kiefer-Salmon test, decomposed into KS1 (skewness) and KS2 (kurtosis)
SR = Studentized Range
Significance levels: * = 10%, ** = 5%, *** = 1%

Table 4.7
Monthly Nominal Dollar Spot Rates
ARCH tests in ΔlnS

ARCH	CD	FF	DM	LIR	YEN	SF	BP
1	1.36	1.75	5.62**	2.11	5.07**	1.64	.01
2	1.36	2.32	7.07**	7.11**	5.96*	1.84	.10
3	1.51	2.62	7.02*	7.36*	6.44*	1.82	.58
4	1.67	2.82	7.52	8.24*	11.72*	2.08	13.17**
8	2.31	3.23	8.71	9.82	19.17*	3.06	12.74
12	7.08	3.21	9.60	12.97	22.16**	6.71	12.64

Significance levels: * 10% **5% *** 1%

Figure 4.1

LOG DM/DOLLAR RATE, END OF MONTH

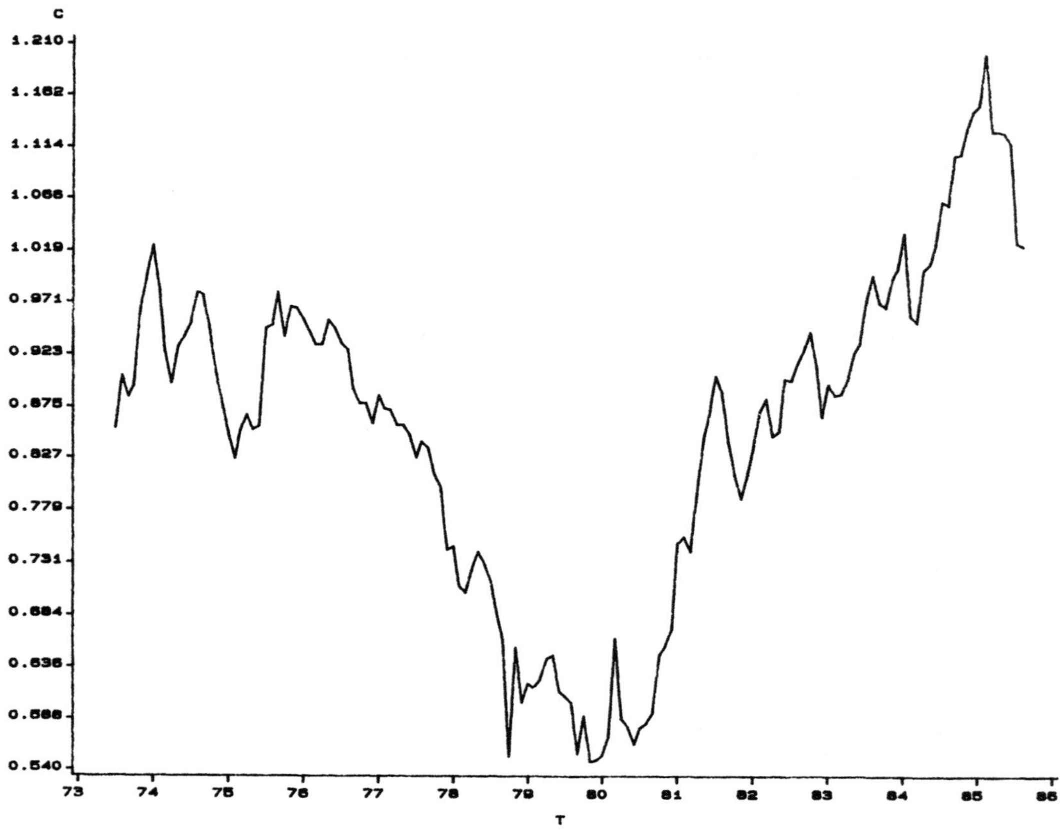

1973–07 THROUGH 1985–08

Figure 4.2
CHANGE IN LOG DM/DOLLAR RATE

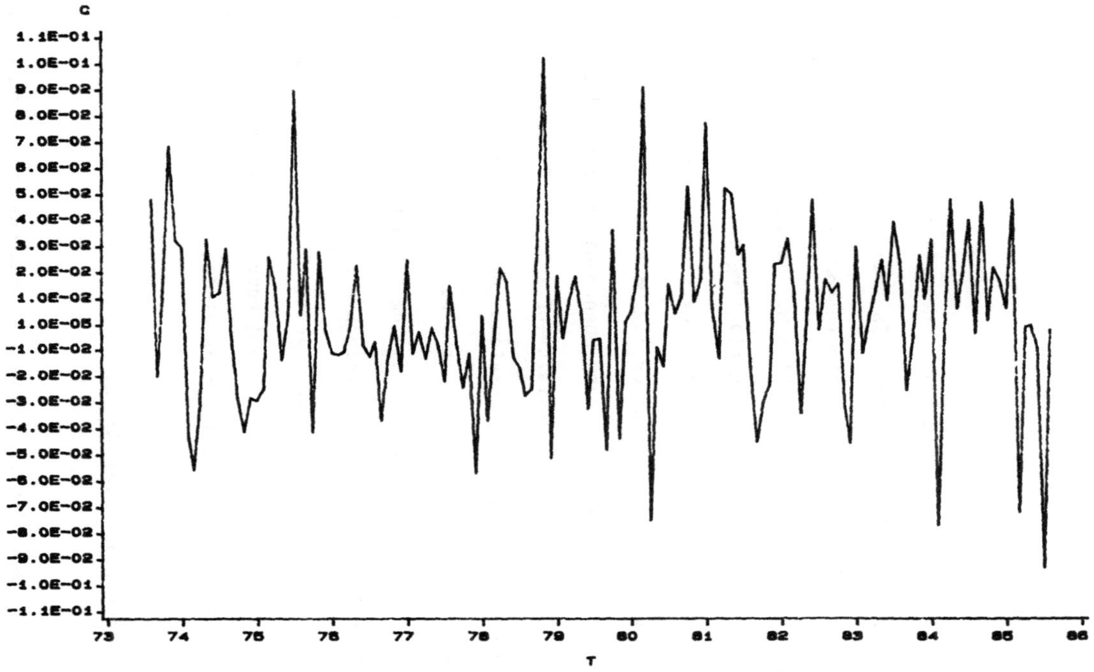

1973-08 THROUGH 1985-08

Chapter Five: Real Exchange Rate Movements

5.1) Introduction

The recent float has led to renewed theoretical and empirical interest in the purchasing power parity (PPP) doctrine. In this chapter we examine the validity of various versions of PPP, in light of the random-walk conditional mean behavior, and ARCH conditional variance behavior, which was documented in earlier chapters for nominal exchange rates. We begin by motivating the absolute and relative versions of the PPP hypothesis in terms of their implications for the behavior of real, as opposed to nominal, exchange rates. In section 5.2 we show that the two PPP hypotheses are intimately related, and argue that many phenomena which may lead directly to failure of absolute PPP need not impare the validity of relative PPP. In section 5.3, the relationship between three key international parity conditions (relative PPP, uncovered interest parity, and real interest parity) is explicitly characterized, and the resulting implications for empirical testing are developed. In section 5.4, the study of deviations from both absolute and relative PPP is motivated in terms of impulse response characteristics of a dynamic system. This sets the stage for the empirical analysis of section 5.5, in which both CPI-based and WPI-based real exchange rate movements are considered. Section 5.6 concludes.

5.2) Forms of Purchasing Power Parity

The arbitrage-based "law of one price", extended to aggregate price levels, is the underlying motivation of aggregate purchasing power parity. Costless instantaneous arbitrage assures uniform pricing (in terms of the same currency) of a common goods basket. Thus, the real exchange rate, given by:

$$R_t = S_t \frac{P_t}{P_t^*} \qquad (5.2.1)$$

is constant and equal to one, where S is the nominal exchange rate in foreign currency units per local currency unit, and P and P^* are the domestic and foreign price levels, respectively. Under absolute PPP, then, we have

$$(5.2.2) \qquad \ln S_t + \ln\left(\frac{P_t}{P_t^*}\right) = 0$$

or

$$(5.2.3) \qquad \ln S_t = \ln\left(\frac{P_t^*}{P_t}\right) .$$

The hypothesis is commonly tested as $(\beta_0, \beta_1) = (0,1)$ in the regression:

$$(5.2.4) \qquad \ln S_t = \beta_0 + \beta_1 \ln\left(\frac{P_t^*}{P_t}\right) + \varepsilon_t .$$

Alternatively, $\ln R_t$ may be viewed as the log deviation from absolute PPP and tested for being zero mean white noise.

Even in a world of optimizing agents, there are many factors which can lead to failure of absolute PPP. The presence of information and transportation costs, price discrimination practices, trade impediments, differences in weights used in the price indexes, systematic differences in productivity levels in the traded and non-traded good sectors, and low substitutability between traded and non-traded goods in consumption and production are common examples.

Thus, attention has shifted from absolute PPP to relative PPP, which postulates that equilibrium changes in exchange rates match inflation rate differentials. It is weak in the sense that it allows for constant transport costs or trade impediments. To see this, suppose that absolute PPP holds only up to a constant:

$$(5.2.5) \qquad \ln S_t = k + \ln\left(\frac{P_t^*}{P_t}\right) .$$

Then relative PPP nevertheless holds:

$$(5.2.6) \qquad \Delta \ln S_t = \Delta \ln\left(\frac{P^*_t}{P_t}\right) .$$

The hypothesis is tested as $(\beta_0, \beta_1) = (0,1)$ in the regression:

$$(5.2.7) \qquad \Delta \ln S_t = \beta_0 + \beta_1 \Delta \ln\left(\frac{P^*_t}{P_t}\right) + \varepsilon_t .$$

Alternatively, $\Delta \ln R_t$ may be viewed as the deviation from relative PPP and tested as zero-mean white noise. Again, many factors such as asymmetric changes in transport costs, commercial policies and nontariff barriers, the weights used for aggregate indexes, and systematic differences in rates of change of productivity in the traded and non-traded good sectors can impair the validity of the theory.

Relative PPP is particularly important because, together with uncovered interest parity and real interest parity, it is one of the three key parity conditions of international economics. We show below that any two of these three conditions implies the third. In particular, relative PPP and uncovered interest parity imply real interest rate parity. If real interest rate parity holds, then small-country monetary policy is rendered impotent in terms of its ability to affect the real rate of interest, and hence saving and investment decisions. In the absence of uncovered interest parity and/or relative PPP, on the other hand, systematic real interest differentials can persist.

5.3) The Relationship Between the Three Parity Conditions

5.3.a) Background

We digress temporarily to characterize the relationship between the three key parity conditions of international economics: uncovered interest rate parity, purchasing power parity, and real interest rate parity. Numerous papers in the literature attempt to independently test these hypotheses; some recent examples are

Cumby and Obstfeld (1981, 1984), Mishkin (1984), and Gaab, Granziol, and Horner (1986). The relationship between the parity conditions is particularly important in light of the random-walk behavior which was documented in Chapters 3 and 4 for nominal exchange rates. If real exchange rates (i.e. deviations from absolute PPP) are found to be similarly nonstationary, we are naturally led to ask what effect, if any, the failure of absolute PPP has on the validity of the other parity conditions.

While each hypothesis is a key element in many exchange rate models, each is also of substantial self-importance. Uncovered interest parity is intimately related to market efficiency, being equivalent to covered interest parity under risk neutrality and market efficiency. Purchasing power parity is important as a fundamental "benchmark" for exchange rate determination or inflation transmission, depending on the exchange rate regime.[1] Real interest rate parity implies that a small country's monetary policy is incapable of influencing its real interest rate. In light of these facts, the attention given to the hypotheses is clearly well-deserved. It is interesting to note, however, that while they are quite interdependent they have received largely separate treatment.

One exception is the common recognition that uncovered interest parity and purchasing power parity imply real interest rate parity. (See Cumby and Obstfeld (1984), inter alia.) It is shown below that the linkages between the hypotheses are actually much more subtle: any two imply the third. This is developed in section 5.3.b, and the results are used to illuminate and interpret some recent findings. Concluding remarks regarding the parity relationships appear in section 5.3.c.

5.3.b) The Parity Conditions

Ex-ante uncovered interest parity (EAUIP) equates nominal interest differentials on k-period bonds with expected rates of nominal exchange rate depreciation over the same period:

---

[1] The "benchmark" role of aggregate PPP, even in light of differential tax structures, different price index baskets, nontradeables, and so forth, is forcefully argued by Dornbusch (1985).

(5.3.1) $$\frac{S^e_{t+k} - S_t}{S_t} = i_{kt} - i^*_{kt},$$

apart from second order terms.

Ex-ante relative purchasing power parity (EAPPP) equates expected k-period inflation rate differentials to expected k-period nominal exchange rate depreciation:

(5.3.2) $$\frac{S^e_{t+k} - S_t}{S_t} = \frac{P^e_{t+k} - P_t}{P_t} - \frac{P^{e*}_{t+k} - P^*_t}{P^*_t}.$$

Ex-ante real interest rate parity (EARIP) is stated as:

(5.3.3) $$r_{k,t} = r^*_{k,t}$$

where

(5.3.4) $$r_{k,t} = i_{kt} - \frac{P^e_{t+k} - P_t}{P_t}.$$

Under rational expectations, of course, the "expectations" in the above formulae are replaced by mathematical expectations conditional on the time-t information set Ω_t. Although all of the results below hold under rational expectations, rationality is in no way required.

It will prove useful to rewrite (5.3.3) as:

(5.3.3') $$i_{kt} - \left(\frac{P^e_{t+k} - P_t}{P_t}\right) = i^*_{kt} - \left(\frac{P^{*e}_{t+k} - P^*_t}{P^*_t}\right).$$

The following proposition is then immediate:

Proposition:

If any two of (5.3.1), (5.3.2), and (5.3.3) is true, then the third is also true. Conversely, if any one of (5.3.1), (5.3.2), and (5.3.3) is false, then one or both of the remaining two is false as well.

Proof:

Subtracting (5.3.2) from (5.3.1) gives (5.3.3). Solving (5.3.3) for $i_{kt} - i^*_{kt}$, and inserting into (5.3.1), gives (5.3.2). Solving (5.3.3) for $\frac{P^e_{t+k} - P_t}{P_t} - \frac{P^*_{t+k} - P_t}{P_t}$, and inserting into (5.3.2), gives (5.3.1).

QED

Stated somewhat differently, the proposition implies that either none, one, or all of the parity conditions must hold. Consider, for example, the earlier-stated fact that EAUIP + EAPPP => EARIP. This corresponds to the simultaneous truth of all three parity conditions. What is less obvious, however, is that neither EAUIP nor EAPPP is necessary for EARIP. As an example, consider Table 5.1, which partially summarizes the results of Cumby and Obstfeld (1984).

Note first that the table largely conforms to our prediction that acceptances can only number 0, 1, or 3. The most common scenario, surprisingly enough, is acceptance of one parity condition and rejection of the other two. In the UK, for example, EARIP appears to hold although both EAUIP and EAPPP fail. The next most common scenario is rejection of all parity conditions. The only theoretically inconsistent result is in line 3 of the table in which German CPI - based EARIP and EAUIP appear to hold, while EAPPP fails.[2]

5.3.c) Conclusions Regarding the Parity Conditions

We have shown that none of the international parity conditions is in any sense more "fundamental" than any other. Any two imply the third, but any or all may be independently asserted. None, one, or all three of them may be true.

---

2 There are a number of explanations for this. First, it may indicate that the WPI, rather than the CPI, is more reasonably used in studies of international parity conditions. This has been argued by Frenkel (1981) in light of the fact that tradeables are more heavily weighted in the WPI. Secondly, and perhaps more importantly 1% significance level used in the table is arbitrary. At the 5% level, line 3 would read:

US/Germany R (CPI) A R 1,

so that the contradiction vanishes.

This has implications for research strategy in international economics. Although the rigorous testing of each parity condition requires sophisticated (and different) econometric tools, direct testing of EARIP is perhaps the most difficult. This suggests, as a first step in research strategy, testing only EAUIP and EAPPP. If those two conditions hold, then EARIP must hold as well.

5.4) On The Stochastic Behavior of Deviations From PPP

In this section we test the validity of absolute and relative PPP by examining the stochastic properties of deviations from absolute PPP. The approach has several advantages relative to least-squares estimation of (5.2.4) and (5.2.7). First, as we show below, the conditional heteroskedasticity found in nominal exchange rates is also present in real rates, due largely to the fact that movements in real rates are dominated by nominal rate movements. This means that tests of (5.2.4) and (5.2.7) will be biased, unless the heteroskedasticity in $\{\varepsilon_t\}$ is controlled for. While this is not difficult, being a direct application of the previously developed ARCH model, it does not allow for direct examination of the temporal pattern of deviations from PPP.

Put differently, the "short run" and "long run" behavior of deviations from PPP may be quite different.[3] In fact, many economists believe that in the long run, PPP is valid and therefore serves as a useful benchmark. Most modern exchange rate models, such as the Dornbusch (1976) overshooting model, and recent attempts to model deviations from PPP (in terms of costly pricing decisions, degree of substitutability of domestic and foreign goods, and exchange rate volatility for a market characterized by monopolistic competition) continue to take long run PPP as the reference point. If this is correct, we have both a "benchmark model" with which to discuss current over-

[3] We use the terms "long run" and "short run" in the sense of impulse response analysis of a dynamic system. A parity condition is said to hold (stochastically) in the short run if deviations from it are uncorrelated noise. A parity condition is said to hold (stochastically) in the long run if deviations from it are serially correlated (but stationary) about a zero mean. A parity condition is said to hold neither in the short run nor the long run if deviations from it are either nonstationary (implying permanent drift) or stationary about a nonzero mean.

or undervaluation of a given currency, and a useful guide for exchange rate expectations formation.

Study of deviations from PPP, after controlling for conditional heteroskedasticity, enables valuable insight into both long-run and short-run behavior. Homogeneous nonstationary (of order one) deviations from absolute PPP imply that they are permanent, even in the long run. Deviations from relative PPP will then be stationary, however, implying that it holds in the long run. (Relative PPP may also hold (stochastically) in the short run, if its heteroskedasticity-controlled deviations display no serial correlation.) Homogeneous nonstationarity of order two in real exchange rates, on the other hand, implies permanent deviations from both absolute and relative PPP.

To crystalize ideas, definitions, and notation, we recap. The log deviation from absolute PPP is given by:

$$\ln R_t = \ln S_t + \ln P_t - \ln P_t^* .$$

The deviation from relative PPP is then immediately $\Delta \ln R_t$ (i.e., the first difference of the log deviation from absolute PPP). If the deviation from absolute PPP is pure white noise (apart from possible ARCH effects, which will be considered shortly), we say that absolute PPP holds (stochastically) in the short run. If the deviations from absolute PPP are not white noise, but nevertheless follow a stationary stochastic process, we say the absolute PPP holds (stochastically) in the long run but not in the short run. If deviations from absolute PPP are trended or integrated (i.e. nonstationary), we say that absolute PPP holds neither in the short run nor in the long run. Identical definitions apply for the deviations from relative PPP, $\Delta \ln R_t$.

The power of this approach stems from two facts. First, the PPP hypotheses are very strong, in the sense that they not only sign partial derivatives, but they actually imply coefficient values. This enables us to work directly in terms of "deviations from PPP". Second, the fact that the deviation from relative PPP is simply the first difference of the deviation from absolute PPP may be put to powerful use, because it enables us to exploit the stochastic structure of absolute PPP deviations to directly characterize the nature of relative PPP deviations.

5.5) Empirical Analysis

We work with the bilateral dollar exchange rates of the major industrial countries: Canada, France, Germany, Italy, Japan, Switzerland and the United Kingdom. Both the consumer price index (CPI) and the wholesale price index (WPI) were used in calculating the inflation rates for PPP testing. Some authors argue that the WPI is more likely to represent tradeable prices and hence is the preferred price series; however, since both indexes have been used in the literature and arguments have been made in favor of both of them, we prefer to remain agnostic on this point.

In fact, following Frenkel (1981), we may use both price indexes to gain some preliminary insight into the likelihood of PPP. In order for PPP to hold, it must be (at least approximately) true that the price of tradeables (P_T) relative to the price of nontradeable (P_N) is constant. If the CPI reflects more nontradeable goods prices and the WPI reflects more tradeable prices, then we can get a rough feel for P_N/P_T by examining the CPI/WPI ratios. Such an analysis indicated near relative price stability for Canada, Germany, Italy, Britain, and the United States. France displayed some relative price movements in the turbulent early years of the float, while Japan and Switzerland showed some movement throughout the period. On the basis of this preliminary analysis, we might expect to see less evidence of PPP, or at least more prolonged deviations from PPP, in the French, Japanese and Swiss cases.

First, it should be noted that the two versions (CPI and WPI) of the log real exchange rate are very similar, the only difference being that the WPI-based series are perhaps slightly more volatile, due to greater volatility in wholesale prices.[4] Second, the movements in real exchange rates closely mimic those of the corresponding nominal

[4] The sample period is again July 1973 through August 1985. The other data details are the same as in Chapter 4, with one exception: for conformity the BP is now in Local/$.

rates. Table 5.2 contains simple correlation coefficients for nominal rates and WPI-based real rates. All correlations are greater than .4; most are greater than .75.

It is clear that comovements of the series are very closely linked, and that nominal movements explain a very large part of real movements. This is due to price "stickiness" and is responsible for the large, persistent, and perhaps nonstationary deviation from absolute PPP which are evident in the graphs.

The formal unit root tests of Tables 5.3 through 5.6 show that there is in fact one unit root in the autoregressive representation of each of the seven log real exchange rates, whether calculated on a CPI or WPI basis. Further joint tests decisively rejected the null of two unit roots. Thus, each log real exchange rate (i.e., deviation from absolute PPP) is homogeneous nonstationary of order one, indicating permanent deviations from absolute PPP, even in the long run. On the other hand, the presence of one, and only one, unit root in each series indicates that the first differences of log real exchange rates (i.e., the deviations from relative PPP) are covariance stationary stochastic processes. This, of course, does not mean that relative PPP holds; rather, it means that it holds at least in the long run, due to the mean reversion of stationary stochastic processes. The first-differenced log real exchange rates (CPI and WPI) are shown in Figures 5.15 to 5.28.

The nature (i.e., temporal structure) of the deviations from relative PPP may be studied by examining the impulse response function of a time-series model fitted to the deviations from relative PPP. We have already examined deviations from absolute PPP and shown that they are nonstationary; we shall shortly examine deviations from relative PPP.

First, however, it is of interest to note that a number of trend terms appear significant in Tables 5.4 and 5.6. This may be due to integrated deviations from quadratic trend, so that a first difference only removes the first-order part of the trend. At any rate, the remaining trend effects are extremely small and are of little economic significance.

The sample autocorrelations of deviations from relative PPP are given in Table 5.7 (CPI-based) and Table 5.8 (WPI-based), in which we see that there is no evidence of serial correlation, much as for the nominal rates. (Even the two "significant" CD sample autocorrelations at lags 11 and 12 are greatly reduced when the WPI is used.) The lack of serial correlation is further confirmed by the distributional statistics in Tables 5.9 and 5.10, which again are very similar to those for monthly nominal rates. In particular, they indicate absence of serial correlation, with symmetric leptokurtic unconditional behavior. Again, the leptokurtosis is greatly reduced relative to those of weekly nominal rates, but roughly identical to that found in monthly nominal rates.

The ARCH tests, reported in Tables 5.11 and 5.12, are roughly identical to those of the monthly nominal rates, with one exception: the conditioning on relative prices has removed the ARCH effects for the LIR. Three remaining major rates (DM, YEN, BP), show significant ARCH effects, however. This means that the serial correlation tests are in fact overly conservative, yet we still can detect no serial correlation.

5.6) Conclusions

We show that monthly real dollar spot exchange rates, like the monthly nominal rates upon which they are based, evolve as approximate random walks and display weak ARCH effects. Thus, deviations from absolute PPP tend to persist, while deviations from relative PPP are approximately uncorrelated noise. The implications of our failure to reject relative PPP for the validity of other parity conditions are discussed; in particular, if we fail to reject one of the other remaining parity conditions, we should fail to reject the third.

Table 5.1
Tests of Parity Conditions#

Relation	EARIP*	EAUIP	EAPPP	Total Acceptances
US/UK	A (CPI)	R	R	1
	A (WPI)		R	1
US/Germany	A (CPI)	A	R	2
	R (WPI)		R	1
US/Switzerland	R (CPI)	A	R	1
	R (WPI)		R	1
US/Canada	R (CPI)	R	R	0
	A (WPI)		R	1
US/Japan	A (CPI)	R	R	1
	R (WPI)		R	0

#Adapted from Cumby and Obstfeld (1984).
* Based on 1 - month eurocurrency rates.
R - Reject at 1% level
A - Accept at 1% level

Table 5.2
Real (WPI-Based) and Nominal Spot Exchange Rate Correlations

Nominal	Real CD	FF	DM	LIR	YEN	SF	BP
CD	.93						
FF		.95					
DM			.78				
LIR				.89			
YEN					.49		
SF						.43	
BP							.51

Table 5.3
Monthly Real (CPI-Based) Dollar Spot Rates
Test For Unit Root in $\ln R_t$, CPI, Nonzero Mean Allowed Under The Alternative

$\Delta \ln R$	const	$\ln R_{-1}$	$\Delta \ln R_{-1}$	$\Delta \ln R_{-2}$	$\Delta \ln R_{-3}$	$\Delta \ln R_{-4}$	$\Delta \ln R_{-5}$
CD	.00183	-.01127	-.12697	-.18165	.10102	.01218	.13702
	(1.47)	(-.72)	(-1.46)	(-2.07)**	(1.13)	(.13)	(1.57)
FF	.00113	-.01249	-.09445	.06763	.05431	.09827	.06070
	(.40)	(-.83)	(-1.10)	(.77)	(.62)	(1.11)	(.69)
DM	.00299	.00208	-.04052	.07073	-.00952	-.05815	-.03003
	(1.01)	(-.14)	(-.46)	(.78)	(-.11)	(-.65)	(-.34)
LIR	.00159	-.01762	-.03303	.02827	.07248	-.04597	.09460
	(.62)	(-.91)	(-.39)	(.33)	(.85)	(-.53)	(1.10)
YEN	-.00019	-.04312	.11711	-.05951	.15053	.01735	.08470
	(-.07)	(-1.98)	(1.36)	(-.68)	(1.75)*	(.20)	(.98)
SF	.00425	-.02719	.02537	.09938	.05309	-.00612	-.00880
	(.97)	(-1.33)	(.29)	(1.10)	(.58)	(-.07)	(-.10)
BP	.00023	-.03151	.05308	.10147	-.05778	.05998	.11412
	(.07)	(-1.62)	(.61)	(1.14)	(-.65)	(.67)	(1.28)

* Significant at 10% Level
** Significant at 5% Level
*** Significant at 2% Level

Table 5.4
Monthly Real CPI-Based Dollar Spot Rates
Test For Unit Root in lnR_t, Trend Allowed Under The Alternative

ΔlnR	const	t	lnR_{-1}	ΔlnR_{-1}	ΔlnR_{-2}	ΔlnR_{-3}	ΔlnR_{-4}	ΔlnR_{-5}
CD	-.00919 (-1.70)*	.00014 (2.10)**	-.07731 (-2.01)	-.09142 (-1.05)	-.15160 (-1.73)*	.12561 (1.41)	.03498 (.40)	.15598 (1.80)*
FF	-.01779 (-2.27)**	.00024 (2.59)**	-.04527 (-2.33)	-.10040 (-1.20)	.05880 (.70)	.05387 (.62)	.09804 (1.13)	.05945 (.69)
DM	-.01516 (-1.73)*	.00023 (2.20)**	-.03575 (-1.70)	-.04028 (-.47)	.06895 (.77)	-.00329 (-.04)	-.05145 (-.58)	-.02807 (-.32)
LIR	-.01331 (-1.87)*	.00019 (2.25)**	-.05661 (-2.20)	-.02263 (-.27)	.03489 (.41)	.08479 (1.00)	-.03051 (-.36)	.10625 (1.25)
YEN	-.00773 (-1.19)	.00009 (1.29)	-.04628 (-2.11)	.11035 (1.29)	-.06849 (-.79)	.14158 (1.64)*	.01078 (.12)	.07661 (.89)
SF	-.00919 (-1.20)	.00020 (2.12)**	-.04633 (-2.10)	.01348 (.16)	.08186 (.91)	.03864 (.43)	-.01876 (-.21)	-.02384 (-.27)
BP	-.00585 (-.85)	.00007 (.98)	-.03273 (-1.68)	.04740 (.55)	.09221 (1.03)	-.64670 (-.72)	.05039 (.56)	.10378 (1.15)

* Significant at 10% Level
** Significant at 5% Level
*** Significant at 2% Level

Table 5.5
Monthly Real (WPI-Based) Dollar Spot Rates
Test For Unit Root in $\ln R_t$, Nonzero Mean Allowed Under the Alternative

$\Delta\ln R$	const	$\ln R_{-1}$	$\Delta\ln R_{-1}$	$\Delta\ln R_{-2}$	$\Delta\ln R_{-3}$	$\Delta\ln R_{-4}$	$\Delta\ln R_{-5}$
CD	.00191	-.03744	-.12247	-.16963	.03467	.02161	.12575
	(1.51)	(-1.86)	(-1.43)	(-1.96)**	(.40)	(.25)	(1.49)
FF	.00278	-.01125	-.13082	.03256	.03134	.04235	.03834
	(.98)	(-.80)	(-1.52)	(.37)	(.35)	(.47)	(.44)
DM	.00244	-.01063	-.01595	.07641	-.04845	-.09204	-.01532
	(.83)	(-.60)	(-.18)	(.85)	(-.55)	(-1.04)	(-.17)
LIR	.00184	-.01537	-.06602	.03703	.02924	-.06722	.07244
	(.71)	(-.80)	(-.76)	(.42)	(.33)	(-.77)	(.83)
YEN	.00131	-.05778	.04856	-.06198	.14280	.05571	.04163
	(.48)	(-1.98)	(.56)	(-.72)	(1.65)*	(.64)	(.48)
SF	.00359	-.02257	.02074	.07924	.00939	-.06068	-.03149
	(.90)	(1.04)	(.24)	(.88)	(.10)	(-.67)	(-.35)
BP	-.00075	-.03964	.06283	.11192	-.10614	.02626	.11627
	(-.25)	(-1.87)	(.73)	(1.26)	(-1.20)	(.30)	(1.32)

* Significant at 10% Level
** Significant at 5% Level
*** Significant at 2% Level

Table 5.6
Monthly Real (WPI-Based) Dollar Spot Rates
Test For Unit Root in $\ln R_t$, Trend Allowed Under The Alternative

$\Delta\ln R$	const	t	$\ln R_{-1}$	$\Delta\ln R_{-1}$	$\Delta\ln R_{-2}$	$\Delta\ln R_{-3}$	$\Delta\ln R_{-4}$	$\Delta\ln R_{-5}$
CD	-.00694	.00011	-.10113	-.07929	-.13010	.06869	.05024	.15028
	(-1.35)	(1.78)*	(-2.47)	(-.90)	(-1.47)	(.77)	(.58)	(1.77)*
FF	-.01887	.00028	-.06221	-.10375	.05498	.05472	.06289	.05356
	(-1.66)*	(1.96)**	(-2.11)	(-1.20)	(.62)	(.61)	(.71)	(.62)
DM	-.01382	.00021	-.04812	-.00593	.08490	-.03387	-.07930	-.00936
	(-1.59)	(1.98)**	(-1.86)	(-.07)	(.95)	(-.39)	(-.90)	(-.11)
LIR	-.01471	.00021	-.06152	-.05089	.04557	.04182	-.05608	.07676
	(-1.86)*	(2.22)**	(-2.18)	(-.59)	(.53)	(.48)	(-.65)	(.90)
YEN	-.00689	.00010	-.07705	.05700	-.05725	.14720	.05956	.04464
	(-1.03)	(1.34)	(-2.37)	(.66)	(-.66)	(1.70)*	(.69)	(.52)
SF	-.01188	.00024	-.06232	.02681	.08203	.01358	-.05479	-.03232
	(-1.48)	(2.21)**	(-2.24)	(.31)	(.92)	(.15)	(-.61)	(-.36)
BP	-.00442	.00004	-.03819	.05904	.10602	-.11056	.02010	.10906
	(-.63)	(.58)	(-1.78)	(.68)	(1.18)	(-1.24)	(.25)	(1.22)

* Significant at the 10% Level
** Significant at the 5% Level
*** Significant at the 1% Level

Table 5.7
Monthly Real (CPI-Based) Dollar Spot Rates
Sample Autocorrelations and Bartlett Standard Errors, ΔlnR

LAG	CD	FF	DM	LIR	YEN	SF	BP
1	-.126 (.083)	-.069 (.083)	-.033 (.083)	-.050 (.083)	.076 (.083)	.013 (.083)	.037 (.083)
2	-.169 (.084)	.072 (.084)	.066 (.084)	.039 (.084)	-.049 (.084)	.076 (.084)	.070 (.084)
3	.116 (.087)	.030 (.087)	.005 (.087)	.056 (.087)	.121 (.087)	.035 (.087)	-.051 (.087)
4	-.008 (.088)	.076 (.088)	-.042 (.088)	-.075 (.088)	.015 (.088)	-.018 (.088)	.041 (.088)
5	.089 (.088)	.058 (.088)	-.017 (.088)	.073 (.088)	.045 (.088)	-.020 (.088)	.078 (.088)
6	-.086 (.088)	-.113 (.088)	-.100 (.088)	-.043 (.088)	-.075 (.088)	-.097 (.088)	-.035 (.088)
7	-.042 (.089)	-.009 (.089)	.027 (.089)	.003 (.089)	-.022 (.089)	.011 (.089)	.016 (.089)
8	.121 (.089)	.006 (.089)	.042 (.089)	-.011 (.089)	.021 (.089)	-.059 (.089)	-.092 (.089)
9	-.053 (.090)	-.024 (.090)	-.033 (.090)	-.051 (.090)	-.030 (.090)	-.013 (.090)	.055 (.090)
10	-.026 (.090)	-.011 (.090)	.072 (.090)	-.026 (.090)	-.055 (.090)	-.042 (.090)	.027 (.090)
11	.238* (.090)	-.005 (.090)	.036 (.090)	-.026 (.090)	.036 (.090)	.073 (.090)	.100 (.090)
12	-.259* (.095)	-.067 (.095)	-.086 (.095)	-.066 (.095)	.139 (.095)	-.024 (.095)	-.015 (.095)

* Exceeds two standard errors

Table 5.8
Monthly Real (WPI-Based) Dollar Spot Rates
Sample Autocorrelations and Bartlett Standard Errors, $\Delta \ln R$

LAG	CD	FF	DM	LIR	YEN	SF	BP
1	-.092	-.134	-.020	-.104	-.017	-.008	.036
	(.083)	(.083)	(.083)	(.083)	(.083)	(.083)	(.083)
2	-.143	.016	.046	.038	-.091	.061	.058
	(.084)	(.084)	(.084)	(.084)	(.084)	(.084)	(.084)
3	.057	-.000	-.031	.021	.112	-.011	-.098
	(.085)	(.085)	(.085)	(.085)	(.085)	(.085)	(.085)
4	.017	.022	-.069	-.099	.004	-.063	.009
	(.086)	(.086)	(.086)	(.086)	(.086)	(.086)	(.086)
5	.099	.052	-.008	.079	-.002	-.034	.080
	(.086)	(.086)	(.086)	(.086)	(.086)	(.086)	(.086)
6	-.091	-.108	-.113	-.033	-.126	-.100	-.052
	(.086)	(.086)	(.086)	(.086)	(.086)	(.086)	(.086)
7	-.035	-.030	-.007	-.052	-.082	-.007	-.001
	(.087)	(.087)	(.087)	(.087)	(.087)	(.087)	(.087)
8	.046	-.022	.019	.004	.040	-.073	-.078
	(.087)	(.087)	(.087)	(.087)	(.087)	(.087)	(.087)
9	-.061	-.006	-.026	-.031	-.052	-.020	.050
	(.087)	(.087)	(.087)	(.087)	(.087)	(.087)	(.087)
10	-.058	.015	.055	-.017	-.075	-.042	.015
	(.088)	(.088)	(.088)	(.088)	(.088)	(.088)	(.088)
11	.160	.060	.067	.012	.067	.088	.134
	(.088)	(.088)	(.088)	(.088)	(.088)	(.088)	(.088)
12	-.189*	-.037	0.064	-.000	.132	-.014	-.010
	(.090)	(.090)	(.090)	(.090)	(.090)	(.090)	(.090)

* Exceeds two standard errors

Table 5.9
Monthly Real (CPI-Based) Dollar Spot Rates
Descriptive Statistics, ΔlnR

	CD	FF	DM	LIR	YEN	SF	BP
LB(6)	10.98*	4.97	2.66	3.00	4.60	2.62	2.70
LB(12)	3.84***	5.82	5.43	4.34	8.68	4.40	6.28
LB(18)	38.58***	8.28	9.35	5.67	17.30	10.96	17.11
M-1	72	72	72	72	72	72	72
MaxP	.003	.008	.008	.006	.008	.009	.011
SumP	.028	.160	.161	.127	.154	.207	.167
FK	7.3050**	3.5551	3.5581	3.2525	3.8217	3.0592	4.5681
Mean	.00151	.03331	.00381	.00218	.00019	.00122	.00059
t (μ=0)	1.29	1.03	1.37	.89	.07	.39	.21
Variance	.00020	.00111	.00112	.00088	.00107	.00144	.00116
Std. Dev.	.01401	.03331	.03347	.02968	.03270	.03789	.03401
CV	930.12	1167.59	878.831	1360.17	17030.1	3112.28	5805.18
Skewness	.88442	.15027	-.00082	.38071	-.01231	.25700	-.59929
Kurtosis	2.80292	1.4733	1.39539	1.29123	1.52199	2.02176	1.32193
D	.11024***	.08856***	.06734	.09816***	.07107*	.08608***	.06173
KS	71.21***	12.56***	9.78***	13.62***	12.33***	24.31***	17.11***
KS1	17.78***	.51	.00	3.36**	.00	1.56	8.49***
KS2	53.43***	12.05***	9.78***	10.26***	12.33***	22.75***	8.61***
Maximum	.06207	.11672	.10502	.09402	.13133	.15820	.08087
Q3	.00806	.02181	.02261	.01445	.01726	.01995	.02413
Median	.00103	.00365	.00391	-.00100	.00233	.00374	.00190
Q1	-.00676	-.01298	-.01514	-.01312	-.01813	-.01783	-.01884
Minimum	-.03069	-.09409	-.10192	-.08210	-.08201	-.11326	-.13538
SR	6.62170**	6.32829*	6.18309*	5.93364	6.52371**	7.16378***	6.35764*

NOTES: LB(N) = Ljung-Box statistic at lag N
M-1 = number of independent periodogram ordinates
MaxP = maximum periodogram ordinate, MinP = minimum periodogram ordinate
SumP = sum of periodogram ordinates
FK = Fisher's kappa
CV = coefficient of variation
D = Kolmogorov's D for the null hypothesis of normality
KS = Kiefer-Salmon normality test, decomposed into KS1 (skewness test) and KS2 (kurtosis test)
SR = Studentized Range
Significance levels: * = 10%, ** = 5%, *** = 1%

Table 5.10
Monthly Real (WPI-Based) Dollar Spot Rates
Descriptive Statistics, $\Delta \ln R_t$

	CD	FF	DM	LIR	YEN	SF	BP
LB(6)	7.58	4.98	3.21	4.50	5.59	2.89	3.52
LB(12)	19.02*	6.01	5.25	5.13	11.71	5.35	7.77
LB(18)	24.60	8.67	7.39	6.92	19.90	9.95	17.51
M-1	72	72	72	72	72	72	72
MaxP	.003	.006	.007	.008	.009	.009	.013
SumP	.031	.151	.169	.128	.149	.214	.176
FK	7.7264**	3.0318	2.799	4.6213	4.1213	3.0422	5.2056
Mean	.00091	.00338	.00303	.00174	.00093	.00196	-.00037
t (μ=0)	.75	1.26	1.06	.70	.35	.61	-.13
Variance	.00022	.00105	.00118	.00089	.00103	.00149	.00122
Std. Dev.	.01471	.03237	.03428	.02986	.03211	.03854	.03493
CV	1615.99	957.95	1132.62	1713.48	3436.71	1967.35	-9404.8
Skewness	.61468	.06063	.03726	-.03519	-.18079	.19392	-.43078
Kurtosis	1.83418	1.78819	1.23021	1.26732	1.08182	1.48586	1.26549
D	.11005***	.10395***	.07758**	.08304**	.09223***	.07268*	.05384
KS	29.89***	17.01***	7.91**	8.25**	6.59**	13.16***	13.08***
KS1	8.83***	.08	.03	.03	.77	.88	4.39**
KS2	21.06***	16.93***	7.88***	8.22***	5.82**	12.28***	8.69***
Maximum	.05490	.10461	.10259	.08687	.11655	.14810	.01813
Q3	.00779	.01635	.02299	.01849	.01881	.02366	.02537
Median	.00093	.00444	.00289	-.00092	.00388	.00416	-.00189
Q1	-.00768	-.01026	-.01434	-.01273	-.01371	-.01838	-.01991
Minimum	-.03729	-.08776	-.09862	-.08527	-.08754	-.10947	-.13966
SR	6.26633*	5.94196	5.86972	5.76586	6.35526*	6.68293**	6.32503*

NOTES: LB(N) = Ljung-Box statistic at lag N
M-1 = number of independent periodogram ordinates
MaxP = maximum periodogram ordinate, MinP = minimum periodogram ordinate
SumP = sum of periodogram ordinates
FK = Fisher's kappa
CV = coefficient of variation
D = Kolmogorov's D for the null hypothesis of normality
KS = Kiefer-Salmon normality test, decomposed into KS1 (skewness test) and KS2 (kurtosis test)
SR = Studentized Range
Significance levels: * = 10%, ** = 5%, *** = 1%

Table 5.11
Monthly Real (CPI-Based) Dollar Spot Rates
ARCH Tests, $\Delta \ln R_t$

ARCH	CD	FF	DM	LIR	YEN	SF	BP
1	1.00	1.64	3.74	.57	2.83	.86	.01
2	1.07	2.23	5.48*	2.27	3.27	.99	1.03
3	1.27	2.86	5.43	3.69	3.26	.98	1.32
4	1.66	3.15	5.88	3.88	8.32*	1.22	10.61**
8	2.77	3.61	7.24	5.63	14.05*	2.04	10.63
12	9.08	3.60	7.95	13.22	14.80	5.39	10.91

Significance levels: * = 10%, ** = 5%, *** = 1%

Table 5.12
Monthly Real (WPI-Based) Dollar Spot Rates
ARCH Tests, $\Delta \ln R_t$

ARCH	CD	FF	DM	LIR	YEN	SF	BP
1	2.02	2.58	3.58*	2.36	2.47	.48	.29
2	2.22	2.90	3.36	2.38	2.47	.61	.54
3	2.52	4.19	5.18	2.54	2.46	.56	1.51
4	2.65	4.57	5.52	2.62	5.05	.90	9.64**
8	4.85	4.32	5.97	4.58	15.76**	1.91	10.32
12	8.01	4.15	6.48	9.97	17.01	5.13	11.38

Significance levels: * = 10%, ** = 5%, *** = 1%

Figure 5.1

LOG CPI--BASED REAL EXCHANGE RATE

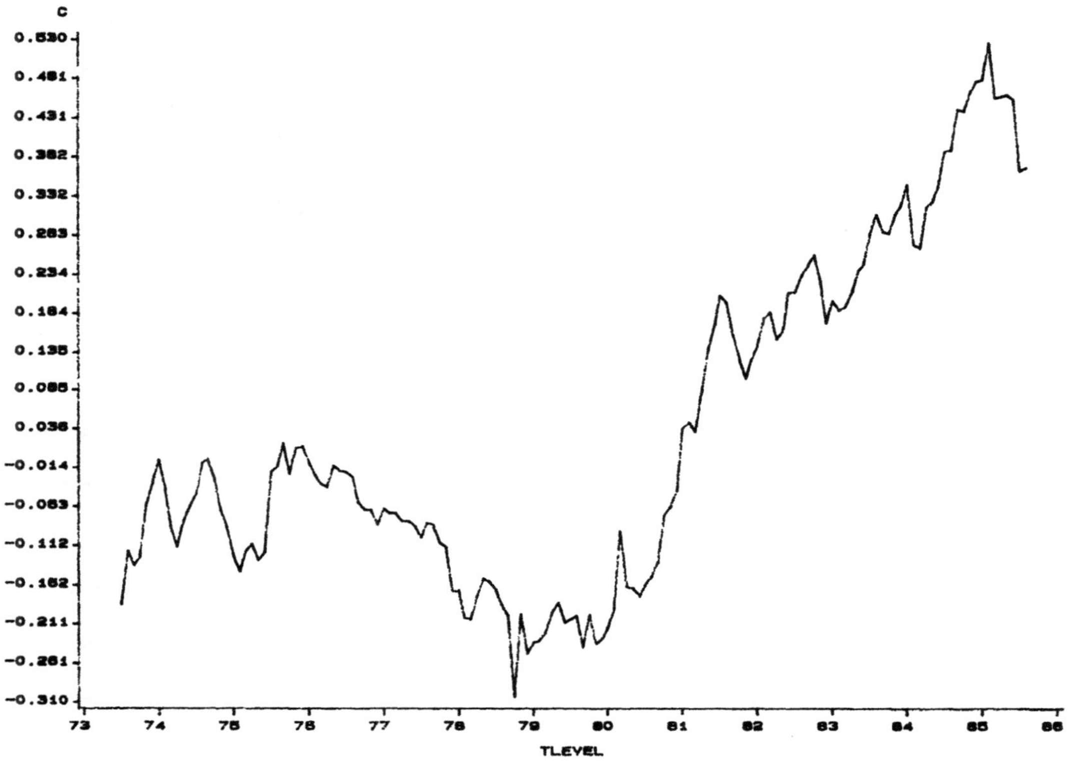

GERMANY

Figure 5.2

LOG WPI–BASED REAL EXCHANGE RATE

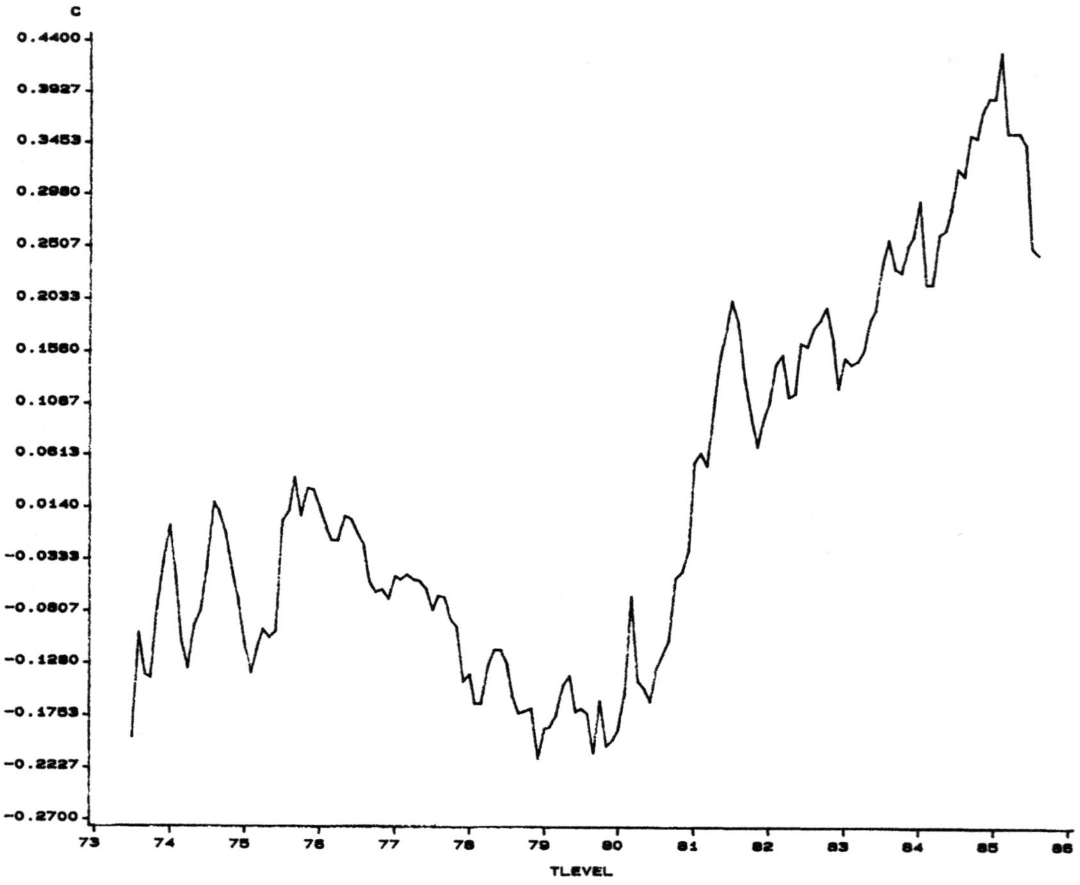

GERMANY

Figure 5.3

CHANGE IN LOG CPI—BASED REAL EXCHANGE RATE

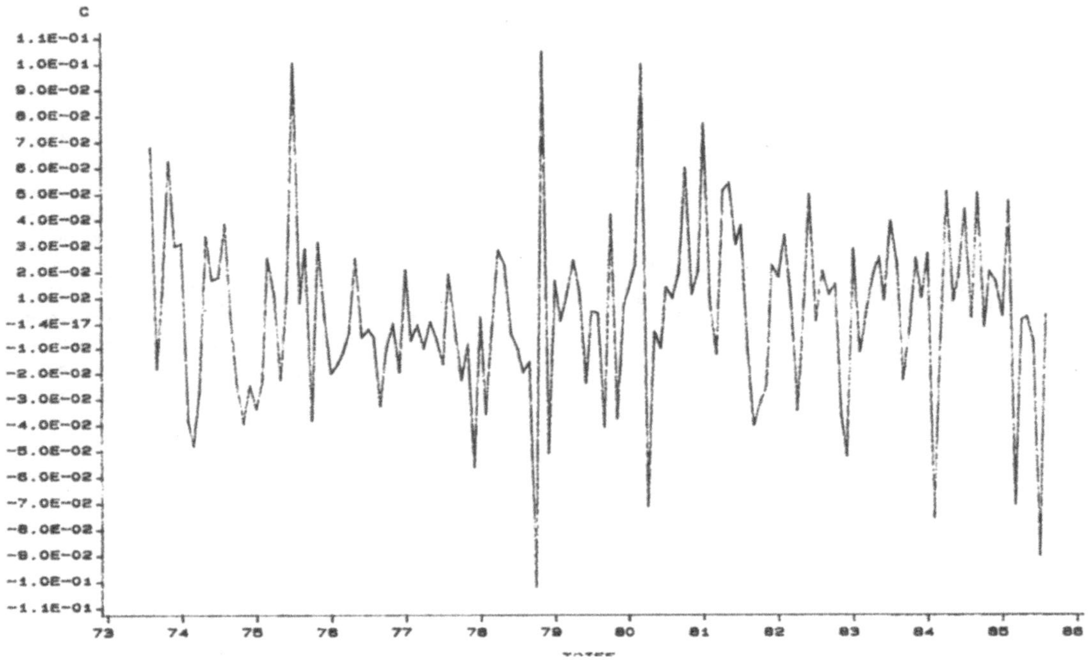

GERMANY

Figure 5.4

CHANGE IN LOG WPI–BASED REAL EXCHANGE RATE

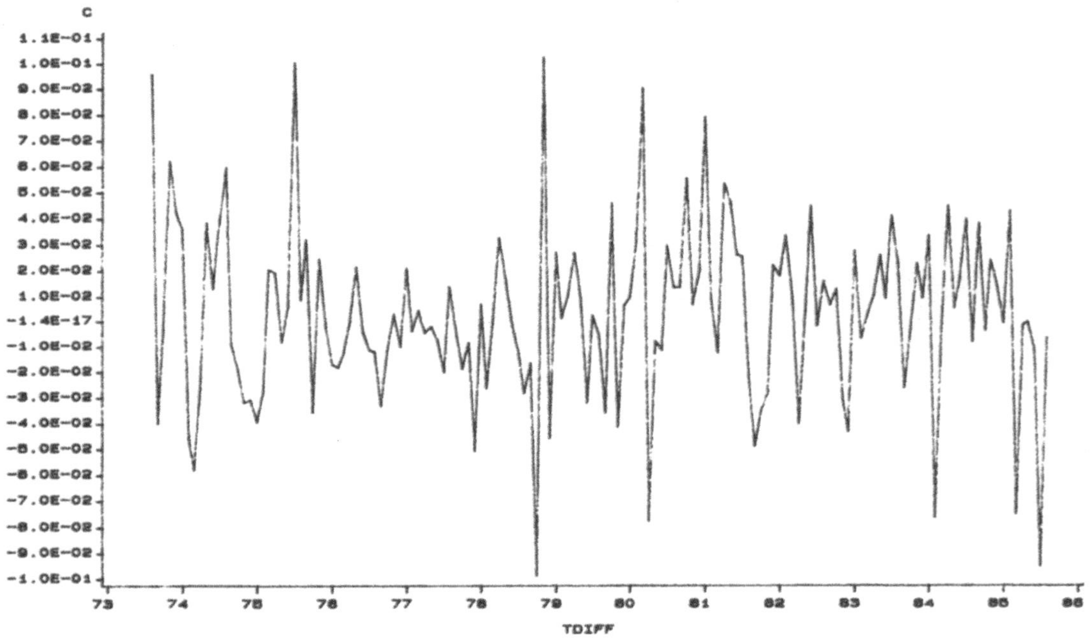

REFERENCES

Akaike, H., 1974, "A New Look at The Statistical Model Identification," IEEE Transactions on Automatic Control, AC-19, 716-723.

Akhtar, M.A., and R.S. Hilton, 1984, "Effects of Exchange Rate Uncertainty on German and U.S. Trade," Research Paper 8403, Federal Reserve Bank of New York.

Amemiya, T. and R.Y. Wu, 1972, "The Effect of Aggregation on Prediction in The Autoregressive Model," Journal of The American Statistical Association, 67, 628-632.

Anderson, R.L. ,1942, "Distribution of the Serial Correlation Coefficient," Annals of Mathematical Statistics, 13, 1-13.

Bachelier, L., 1900, Theorie de la Speculation, Paris: Gauthier-Villars. Reprinted in Cootner, P. (ed.) The Random Character of Stock Market Prices, Cambridge: MIT Press, 1964, p. 17-78.

Barone-Adesi, G. and P.P. Talwar, 1983, "Market Models and Heteroskedasticity of Residual Security Returns," Journal of Business and Economic Statistics, 1, 163-168.

Bartlett, M.S., 1946, "On The Theoretical Specification of Sampling Properties of Autocorrelated Time Series," Journal of The Royal Statistical Society, Series B, 8, 27-41.

Bell, W.R., and S.C. Hillmer, 1984, "Issues Involved with the Seasonal Adjustment of Economic Time Series," Journal of Business and Economic Statistics, 4, 291-320.

Bergstrand, J.H., 1983, "Is Exchange Rate Volatility 'Excessive'?," New England Economic Review, September, 5-14.

Bey, R.P. and G.E. Pinches, 1980, "Additional Evidence of Heteroskedasticity in the Market Model," Journal of Financial and Quantitative Analysis, 15, 299-322.

Bilson, J.F.O., 1979, "The DM/$ Rate: A Monetary Analysis," in K. Brunner and A. Meltzer, eds., Policies For Employment, Prices, and Exchange Rates, Carnegie-Rochester Conference 11, Amsterdam: North Holland.

Box, G.E.P., and G.M. Jenkins, 1970, Time Series Analysis, Forecasting And Control, San Francisco: Holden-Day.

Box, G.E.P., and D.A. Pierce, 1970, "Distribution of The Residual Autocorrelations in ARIMA Time Series Models," Journal of The American Statistical Association, 65, 1509-1526.

Breusch, T., and A.R. Pagan, 1980, "The Lagrange Multiplier Test and Its Application to Model Specification in Econometrics," Review of Economic Studies, 17, 239-253.

Brewer, K.R.W. (1973) "Some Consequences of Temporal Aggregation and Systematic Sampling for ARMA and ARMAX Models," Journal of Econometrics, 1, 133-154.

Callen, J.L., C.Ç.Y. Kwan, and P.C.Y. Yip, 1985, "Foreign Exchange Rate Dynamics: An Empirical Study Using Maximum Entropy Spectral Analysis," Journal of Business and Economic Statistics, 3, 149-155.

Clark, P.K., 1973, "A Subordinated Stochastic Process Model with Finite Variance for Speculative Prices," Econometrica, 41, 135-156.

Cleveland, W.P., and G.C. Tiao, 1976, "Decomposition of Seasonal Time Series: A Model For The Census X-11 Program," Journal of the American Statistical Association, 71, 581-587.

Cornell, B., 1977, "Spot Rates, Forward Rates, And Exchange Market Efficiency," Journal of Financial Economics, 5, 55-65.

Cumby, R.E. and M. Obstfeld, 1984, "International Interest Rate and Price Level Linkages Under Flexible Exchange Rates: A Review of Recent Evidence," in J.F.O. Bilson and R.C. Marston (eds.) Exchange Rate Theory and Practice. Chicago: University of Chicago Press.

Cumby, R.E. and M. Obstfeld, 1981, "A Note on Exchange Rate Expectations and Nominal Interest Differentials: A Test of the Fisher Hypothesis," Journal of Finance, 36, 697-704.

Cushman, D.O., 1983, "The Effects of Real Exchange Rate Risk on International Trade," Journal of International Economics, 15, 45-63.

Dickey, D.A., 1976, "Hypothesis Testing For Nonstationary Time Series," Unpublished Ph.D. Dissertation, Iowa State University, Ames, Iowa.

Dickey, D.A., 1984, "Powers of Unit Root Tests," Proceedings of the American Statistical Association, Business and Economic Statistics Section.

Dickey, D.A., W.R. Bell and R.M. Miller, 1986, "Unit Roots in Time Series Models: Tests and Implications," American Statistician, 40, 12-26.

Dickey, D.A and Fuller, W.A., 1979, "Distribution of the Estimators for Autoregressive Time Series With a Unit Root," Journal of the American Statistical Association, 74.

Diebold, F.X., C.W.J. Lee, and J. Im, 1985, "A New Approach to the Detection and Treatment of Heteroskedasticity in the Market Model," Working Paper, University of Pennsylvania.

Diebold, F.X. and M. Nerlove, 1985, "ARCH Models of Exchange Rate Fluctuations," Paper presented at the 1985 NBER-NSF Conference on Time Series Analysis.

Diebold, F.X., 1986a, "The Time-Series Structure of Exchange Rate Fluctuations," Ph.D. Dissertation, University of Pennsylvania.

Diebold, F.X., 1986b, "Modeling Persistence in Conditional Variances: A Comment," Econometrics Reviews, 51-56.

Diebold, F.X., 1986c, "Testing for Serial Correlation in the Presence of ARCH," Proceedings of the American Statistical Association, Business and Economic Statistics Section, 323-328, Washington, DC: American Statistical Association.

Diebold, F.X., 1986d, "Temporal Aggregation of ARCH Processes and the Distribution of Asset Returns," Special Studies Paper, #200, Board of Governors of the Federal Reserve System.

Diebold, F.X., 1986e, "Rational Expectations, Random Walks, and Monetary Models of the Exchange Rate, "Proceedings of the American Statistical Association, Business and Economic Statistics Section, 101-106, Washington, DC: American Statistical Association.

Diebold, F.X. and M. Nerlove, 1986f, "The Dynamics of Exchange Rage Volatility: A Multivariate Latent-Factor ARCH Model," Special Studies Paper, 205, Federal Reserve Board.

Diebold, F.X., and P. Pauly, 1985, "Evidence on the Small Sample Properties of Some Asymptotically Equivalent Tests For Autoregressive Conditional Heteroskedasticity," Econometrics Working Paper #85-01, University of Pennsylvania.

Diebold, F.X. and P. Pauly, 1986g, "Endogenous Risk in a Rational Expectations Portfolio-Balance Model of the DM/Dollar Rate," Forthcoming, European Economic Review.

Domowitz, I. and C.S Hakkio, 1983, "Testing for Serial Correlation in the Presence of Heteroskedasticity with Applications to Exchange Rate Models," Working Paper, Northwestern University.

Domowitz, I. and C.S. Hakkio, 1985, "Conditional Variance and the Risk Premium in the Foreign Exchange Market," Journal of International Economics, 19, 47-66.

Dornbusch, R., 1976, "Expectations And Exchange Rate Dynamics," Journal of Political Economy, 84, 1161-1176.

Dornbusch, R., 1985, "Purchasing Power Parity," NBER Working Paper #1591, forthcoming in The New Palgrave.

Durbin, J., 1970, "Testing for Serial Correlation in Least Squares Regression When Some of the Regressors are Lagged Dependent Variables," Econometrica, 38, 410-421.

Engle, R.F., 1982a, "A General Approach to Lagrange Multiplier Model Diagnostics," Journal of Econometrics, 21, 83-104.

Engle, R.F., 1982b, "Autoregressive Conditional Heteroskedasticity With Estimates of The Variance of U.K. Inflation," Econometrica, 50, 987-1008.

Engle, R.F., 1982c, "Estimates of the Variance of US Inflation Based on the ARCH Model," Journal of Money, Credit and Banking, 15, 286-301.

Engle, R.F. and T. Bollerslev, 1986, "Measuring the Persistance in Conditional Variances," Econometric Reviews, 5, 1-50.

Engle, R.F., D.M. Lillien and R.P. Robins, 1987, "Estimating Time-Varying Risk Premia in the Term Structure: The ARCH-M Model," Econometrica, 55.

Evans, G.B.A. and N.E. Savin, 1981, "Testing for Unit Roots I," Econometrica, 49.

Fama, E.F., 1965, "The Behavior of Stock Market Prices," Journal of Business, 38, 34-105.

Fama, E.F., 1976, Foundations of Finance, New York: Basic Books.

Fama, E.F., and R. Roll, 1968, "Some Properties of Symmetric Stable Distributions," Journal of the American Statistical Association, 63, 817-836.

Fama, E.F., and R. Roll, 1971, "Parameter Estimates for Symmetric Stable Distributions," Journal of the American Statistical Association, 66, 331-338.

Fisher, R.A., 1929, "Tests of Significance in Harmonic Analysis," Proc. Roy. Soc. London, Ser. A, 125, 54-59.

Fletcher, R., 1970, "A New Approach to Variable Metric Algorithms," Computer Journal, 13.

Frenkel, J.A., 1979, "On The Mark: A Theory of Floating Exchange Rates Based on Real Interest Differentials," American Economic Review, 69, 610-622.

Frenkel, J.A., 1976, "A Monetary Approach To The Exchange Rate: Doctrinal Aspects And Empirical Evidence," Scandinavian Journal of Economics, 78, 200-224.

Frenkel, J.A., 1981a, "Flexible Exchange Rates, Prices And The Role of News: Lessons From The 1970's," Journal of Political Economy, 89, 665-705.

Frenkel, J.A., 1981b, "The Collapse of Purchasing Power Parities during the 1970's," European Economic Review, 16, 145-165.

Frenkel, J.A., and M. Mussa, 1980, "The Efficiency of Foreign Exchange Markets and Measures of Turbulence," American Economic Review, 70, 374-381.

Friedman, M., 1953, "The Case for Flexible Exchange Rates," in Essays in Positive Economics, Chicago: University of Chicago Press.

Fuller, W.A., 1976, Introduction To Statistical Time Series, New York: John Wiley and Sons.

Gaab, W., Granziol, M.J. and Horner, M. (1986), "On Some International Parity Conditions: An Empirical Investigation," European Economic Review.

Giacotto, C. and M.M. Ali, 1982, "Optimum Distribution-Free Tests and Further Evidence of Heteroskedasticity in the Market Model," Journal of Finance, 37, 1247-1257.

Giacotto, C. and M.M. Ali, 1985, "Optimum Distribution-Free Tests and Further Evidence of Heteroskedasticity in the Market Model: Reply," Journal of Finance, 40, 607-608.

Godfrey, L.G., 1978, "Testing for Higher Order Serial Correlation in Regression Equations When the Regressors Include Lagged Dependent Variables," Econometrica, 46, 1303-1310.

Godfrey, L.G., 1979, "Testing the Adequacy of a Time-Series Model," Biometrika, 66, 67-72.

Granger, C.W.J., and P. Newbold, 1977, Forecasting Economic Time Series, New York: Academic Press.

Grether, D.M., and M. Nerlove, 1970, "Some Properties of 'Optimal' Seasonal Adjustment," Econometrica, 38, 682-703.

Hannan, E.J., 1970, Multiple Time Series, New York: John Wiley and Sons.

Hannan, E.J., 1980, "The Estimation of The Order of an ARMA Process," Annals of Statistics, 8, 1071-1081.

Hasza, D.P. and W.A. Fuller, 1979, "Estimation for Autoregressive Processes With Unit Roots," Annals of Statistics, 7, 1106-1120.

Hooper, P., and S.W. Kohlhagen, 1978, "The Effect of Exchange Rate Uncertainty on the Prices and Volume of International Trade," Journal of International Economics, 8, 483-512.

Hooper. P. and J.E. Morton, 1982, Fluctuations in The Dollar: A Model of Nominal And Real Exchange Rate Determination," Journal of International Money And Finance, 1, 39-56.

Huang, R.D., 1981, "The Monetary Approach to Exchange Rates in an Efficient Market: Tests Based on Volatility," Journal of Finance, 36, 31-42.

International Monetary Markets Yearbook, Chicago Mercantile Exchange, various issues.

Johnson, H., 1969, "The Case for Flexible Exchange Rates, 1969," Federal Reserve Bank of St. Louis Review, 51, 12-24.

Joreskog, K.G., 1979, "Author's Addendum to: A General Approach to Confirmatory Factor Analysis," in K.G. Joreskog and D. Sorbom (eds.), Advances in Factor Analysis and Structural Equation Models, Cambridge, Mass.: Abt Books.

Kendall, M. and A. Stuart, 1977, The Advanced Theory of Statistics, Volume 1, London: C. Griffin & Co.

Kennen, P.B., and D. Rodrick, 1985, "Measuring and Analyzing the Effects of Short Term Volatility in Real Exchange Rates," Working paper, Princeton University.

Kiefer, N.M., and M. Salmon, 1983, "Testing Normality in Econometric Models," Economics Letters, 11, 123-127.

Kraft, D.F. and R.F. Engle, 1982, "ARCH in Multiple Time-Series Models," Working Paper #82-23, UCSD.

Kreinin, M.E., 1977, "The Effect of Exchange Rate Changes on the Prices and Volume of Foreign Trade," IMF Staff Papers, 24, 297-329.

Lanyi, A., and E.C. Suss, 1982, "Exchange Rate Variability: Alternative Measures and Interpretation," IMF Staff Papers, 29, 527-560.

Levich, R., 1985, "Empirical Studies of Exchange Rates: Price, Behavior, Rate Determination, and Market Efficiency," in Handbook of International Economics. (R.W. Jones and P.B. Kenen, eds.), Amsterdam: North Holland.

Lintner, J., 1965, "Security Prices, Risk, and the Maximal Gains From Diversification," Journal of Finance, 20, 587-616.

Ljung, G.M., and G.E.P. Box, 1978, "On a Measure of Lack of Fit in Time-Series Models," Biometrika, 65, 297-303.

Mandelbrot, B., 1963, "The Variation of Certain Speculative Prices," Journal of Business, 36, 394-419.

Martin, J.D. and R. Klemosky, 1975, "Evidence of Heteroskedasticity in the Market Model," Journal of Business, 48, 1-86.

McCurdy, T. and G.I. Morgan, 1985, "Testing the Martingale Hypothesis in the DM/$ Futures and Spot Markets," Queen's University discussion paper #639.

McNees, S.S., 1979, "The Forecasting Record For The 1970's," New England Economic Review, 33-53.

Meese, R.A., and K. Rogoff, 1983a, "Empirical Exchange Rate Models of The Seventies: Do They Fit Out of Sample?," Journal of International Economics, 14, 3-24.

Meese, R.A., and K. Rogoff, 1983b, "The Out of Sample Failure of Empirical Exchange Rate Models: Sampling Error or Misspecification?," in J. Frenkel, ed., Exchange Rates And International Economics, Chicago: University of Chicago Press.

Meese, R.A., and K.J. Singleton, 1982, "On Unit Roots And The Empirical Modeling of Exchange Rates," Journal of Finance, 37, 1029-1035.

Milhoj, A. ,1985, "The Moment Structure of ARCH Processes," Scandanavian Journal of Statistics, 12, 281-292.

Mishkin, F.S., 1984, "Are Real Interest Rates Equal Across Countries? An Empirical Investigation of International Parity Conditions," Journal of Finance, 39, 1345-1358.

Mussa, M. ,1979, "Empirical Regularities in The Behavior of Exchange Rates and Theories of The Foreign Exchange Market," in K. Brunner, and A. Meltzer, eds., Policies For Employment, Prices And Exchange Rates, Carnegie Rochester Conference #11, Amsterdam: North Holland.

Nemec, A.F.L., 1985, "Conditionally Heteroskedastic Autoregressions," Technical Report #43, Department of Statistics, University of Washington.

Nerlove, M., D.M. Grether, and J.L. Carvalho, 1979, Analysis of Economic Time Series: A Synthesis, New York: Academic Press.

Obstfeld, M. and A.C. Stockman, 1983, "Exchange Rate Dynamics," in R.W. Jones & P.B. Kenen (eds.), Handbook of International Economics, Vol. II, Amsterdam: North-Holland.

Pantula, S.G., 1985, "Estimation of Autoregressive Models with ARCH Errors," Working Paper, Department of Statistics, North Carolina State University.

Poole, W.P., 1966, "The Canadian Experiment With Flexible Exchange Rates, 1950-62," Ph.D. Dissertation, University of Chicago.

Poole, W.P., 1967, "Speculative Prices as Random Walks: An Analysis of Ten Time Series of Flexible Exchange Rates," Southern Economic Journal, 33, 468-478.

Rao, C.R., 1973, Linear Statistical Inference and Its Applications, New York: John Wiley.

Said, S.E., and D.A. Dickey, 1984, "Testing for Unit Roots in ARMA Models of Unknown Order," Biometrika, 71, 599-607.

Schwarz, G., 1978, "Estimating The Dimension of a Model," Annals of Statistics, 6, 461-464.

Sharpe, W.F., 1964, "Capital Asset Prices: A Theory of Market Equilibrium Under Conditions of Risk," Journal of Finance, 19, 425-442.

Solo, V., 1984, "The Order of Differencing in ARIMA Models," Journal of The American Statistical Association, 79: 916-921.

Stewart, G.W., 1967, "A Modification of Davidon's Minimization Method to Accept Difference Approximations," Journal of the Association for Computing Machinery, 14.

Tsay, R., 1987, "ARCH and Time-Varying Parameter Models," Journal of The American Statistical Association.

Watson, M. and R.F. Engle, 1983, "Alternative Algorithms for the Estimation of Dynamic Factor, MIMIC, and Time-Varying Coefficient Models," Journal of Econometrics, 15, 385-400.

Weiss, A.A., 1984, "ARMA Models With ARCH Errors," Journal of Time Series Analysis, 5, 129-143.

Weiss, A.A., 1986, "Asymptotic Theory for ARCH Models: Stability, Estimation and Testing," Econometric Theory, 2, 107-131.

Westerfield, J.M., 1977, "An Examination of Foreign Exchange Risk Under Fixed And Floating Rate Regimes," Journal of International Economics, 7, 181-200.

White, H., 1982, "A Heteroskedasticity-Consistent Covariance Matrix Estimator and a Direct Test For Heteroskedasticity," Econometrica, 48, 817-838.

White, H., 1984, Asymptotic Theory for Econometricians, New York: Academic Press.

White, J.S., 1959, "The Limiting Distribution of the Serial Correlation Coefficient in the Explosive Case II," Annals of Mathematical Statistics, 30.

Wichern, D.W., 1973, "The Behavior of The Sample Autocorrelation Function of an Integrated Moving Average Process," Biometrika, 60, 235-239.

Working, H., 1960, "A Note on The Correlation of First Differences in a Random Chain," Econometrica, 28, 916-918.

Zis, G., 1983, "Exchange Rate Fluctuations, 1973-1982," National Westminster Bank Quarterly Review, August, 2-13.

Vol. 211: P. van den Heuvel, The Stability of a Macroeconomic System with Quantity Constraints. VII, 169 pages. 1983.

Vol. 212: R. Sato and T. Nôno, Invariance Principles and the Structure of Technology. V, 94 pages. 1983.

Vol. 213: Aspiration Levels in Bargaining and Economic Decision Making. Proceedings, 1982. Edited by R. Tietz. VIII, 406 pages. 1983.

Vol. 214: M. Faber, H. Niemes und G. Stephan, Entropie, Umweltschutz und Rohstoffverbrauch. IX, 181 Seiten. 1983.

Vol. 215: Semi-Infinite Programming and Applications. Proceedings, 1981. Edited by A. V. Fiacco and K. O. Kortanek. XI, 322 pages. 1983.

Vol. 216: H. H. Müller, Fiscal Policies in a General Equilibrium Model with Persistent Unemployment. VI, 92 pages. 1983.

Vol. 217: Ch. Grootaert, The Relation Between Final Demand and Income Distribution. XIV, 105 pages. 1983.

Vol. 218: P. van Loon, A Dynamic Theory of the Firm: Production, Finance and Investment. VII, 191 pages. 1983.

Vol. 219: E. van Damme, Refinements of the Nash Equilibrium Concept. VI, 151 pages. 1983.

Vol. 220: M. Aoki, Notes on Economic Time Series Analysis: System Theoretic Perspectives. IX, 249 pages. 1983.

Vol. 221: S. Nakamura, An Inter-Industry Translog Model of Prices and Technical Change for the West German Economy. XIV, 290 pages. 1984.

Vol. 222: P. Meier, Energy Systems Analysis for Developing Countries. VI, 344 pages. 1984.

Vol. 223: W. Trockel, Market Demand. VIII, 205 pages. 1984.

Vol. 224: M. Kiy, Ein disaggregiertes Prognosesystem für die Bundesrepublik Deutschland. XVIII, 276 Seiten. 1984.

Vol. 225: T. R. von Ungern-Sternberg, Zur Analyse von Märkten mit unvollständiger Nachfragerinformation. IX, 125 Seiten. 1984

Vol. 226: Selected Topics in Operations Research and Mathematical Economics. Proceedings, 1983. Edited by G. Hammer and D Pallaschke. IX, 478 pages. 1984.

Vol. 227: Risk and Capital. Proceedings, 1983. Edited by G. Bamberg and K. Spremann. VII, 306 pages. 1984.

Vol. 228: Nonlinear Models of Fluctuating Growth. Proceedings, 1983. Edited by R. M. Goodwin, M. Krüger and A. Vercelli. XVII, 277 pages. 1984.

Vol. 229: Interactive Decision Analysis. Proceedings, 1983. Edited by M. Grauer and A. P. Wierzbicki. VIII, 269 pages. 1984.

Vol. 230: Macro-Economic Planning with Conflicting Goals. Proceedings, 1982. Edited by M. Despontin, P. Nijkamp and J. Spronk. VI, 297 pages. 1984.

Vol. 231: G. F. Newell, The M/M/∞ Service System with Ranked Servers in Heavy Traffic. XI, 126 pages. 1984.

Vol. 232: L. Bauwens, Bayesian Full Information Analysis of Simultaneous Equation Models Using Integration by Monte Carlo. VI, 114 pages. 1984.

Vol. 233: G. Wagenhals, The World Copper Market. XI, 190 pages 1984.

Vol. 234: B. C. Eaves, A Course in Triangulations for Solving Equations with Deformations. III, 302 pages. 1984.

Vol. 235: Stochastic Models in Reliability Theory. Proceedings, 1984. Edited by S. Osaki and Y. Hatoyama. VII, 212 pages. 1984.

Vol. 236: G. Gandolfo, P. C. Padoan, A Disequilibrium Model of Real and Financial Accumulation in an Open Economy. VI, 172 pages. 1984.

Vol. 237: Misspecification Analysis. Proceedings, 1983. Edited by T. K. Dijkstra. V, 129 pages. 1984.

Vol. 238: W. Domschke, A. Drexl, Location and Layout Planning. IV, 134 pages. 1985.

Vol. 239: Microeconomic Models of Housing Markets. Edited by K. Stahl. VII, 197 pages. 1985.

Vol. 240: Contributions to Operations Research. Proceedings, 1984. Edited by K. Neumann and D. Pallaschke. V, 190 pages. 1985.

Vol. 241: U. Wittmann, Das Konzept rationaler Preiserwartungen. XI, 310 Seiten. 1985.

Vol. 242: Decision Making with Multiple Objectives. Proceedings, 1984. Edited by Y. Y. Haimes and V. Chankong. XI, 571 pages. 1985.

Vol. 243: Integer Programming and Related Areas. A Classified Bibliography 1981–1984. Edited by R. von Randow. XX, 386 pages. 1985.

Vol. 244: Advances in Equilibrium Theory. Proceedings, 1984. Edited by C. D. Aliprantis, O. Burkinshaw and N. J. Rothman. II, 235 pages. 1985.

Vol. 245: J. E. M. Wilhelm, Arbitrage Theory. VII, 114 pages. 1985.

Vol. 246: P. W. Otter, Dynamic Feature Space Modelling, Filtering and Self-Tuning Control of Stochastic Systems. XIV, 177 pages. 1985.

Vol. 247: Optimization and Discrete Choice in Urban Systems. Proceedings, 1983. Edited by B. G. Hutchinson, P. Nijkamp and M. Batty. VI, 371 pages. 1985.

Vol. 248: Plural Rationality and Interactive Decision Processes. Proceedings, 1984. Edited by M. Grauer, M. Thompson and A. P. Wierzbicki. VI, 354 pages. 1985.

Vol. 249: Spatial Price Equilibrium: Advances in Theory, Computation and Application. Proceedings, 1984. Edited by P. T. Harker. VII, 277 pages. 1985.

Vol. 250: M. Roubens, Ph. Vincke, Preference Modelling. VIII, 94 pages. 1985.

Vol. 251: Input-Output Modeling. Proceedings, 1984. Edited by A. Smyshlyaev. VI, 261 pages. 1985.

Vol. 252: A. Birolini, On the Use of Stochastic Processes in Modeling Reliability Problems. VI, 105 pages. 1985.

Vol. 253: C. Withagen, Economic Theory and International Trade in Natural Exhaustible Resources. VI, 172 pages. 1985.

Vol. 254: S. Müller, Arbitrage Pricing of Contingent Claims. VIII, 151 pages. 1985.

Vol. 255: Nondifferentiable Optimization: Motivations and Applications. Proceedings, 1984. Edited by V. F. Demyanov and D. Pallaschke. VI, 350 pages. 1985.

Vol. 256: Convexity and Duality in Optimization. Proceedings, 1984. Edited by J. Ponstein. V, 142 pages. 1985.

Vol. 257: Dynamics of Macrosystems. Proceedings, 1984. Edited by J.-P. Aubin, D. Saari and K. Sigmund. VI, 280 pages. 1985.

Vol. 258: H. Funke, Eine allgemeine Theorie der Polypol- und Oligopolpreisbildung. III, 237 pages. 1985.

Vol. 259: Infinite Programming. Proceedings, 1984. Edited by E. J. Anderson and A. B. Philpott. XIV, 244 pages. 1985.

Vol. 260: H.-J. Kruse, Degeneracy Graphs and the Neighbourhood Problem. VIII, 128 pages. 1986.

Vol. 261: Th. R. Gulledge, Jr., N. K. Womer, The Economics of Made-to-Order Production. VI, 134 pages. 1986.

Vol. 262: H. U. Buhl, A Neo-Classical Theory of Distribution and Wealth. V, 146 pages. 1986.

Vol. 263: M. Schäfer, Resource Extraction and Market Structure. XI, 154 pages. 1986.

GPSR Compliance

The European Union's (EU) General Product Safety Regulation (GPSR) is a set of rules that requires consumer products to be safe and our obligations to ensure this.

If you have any concerns about our products, you can contact us on ProductSafety@springernature.com

In case Publisher is established outside the EU, the EU authorized representative is:

Springer Nature Customer Service Center GmbH
Europaplatz 3
69115 Heidelberg, Germany

Batch number: 10844827

Printed by Printforce, the Netherlands